# _God's Blueprint for Spiritual Growth and Reward!_

## _(THE MOSAIC TABERNACLE)_
## _~ First Revision ~_

### _By Pastor Steve Morgan_

*Our mission is to efficiently provide the world's finest, most comprehensive book publishing
service, enabling every author to experience success. To find out how to publish your book,
your way, and have it available worldwide, visit us online at www.trafford.com*

*Trafford rev. 09/14/2010*

 www.trafford.com

**North America & international**
toll-free: 1 888 232 4444 (USA & Canada)
phone: 250 383 6864 ♦ fax: 812 355 4082

# *ENDORSEMENTS*

*Pastor Steve Morgan has proven to be a man with prolific understanding of the Mosaic Tabernacle. The eyes of his understanding have been enlightened by the Spirit of God with such insight and practical teaching to help us walk in the light of our redemption. His revelation of the Tabernacle reveals Jesus Christ as Lord and how it applies in a pragmatic way of our being in him. For it's in Him that we live and move and have our being. It's All About Him in the Courtyard, the Holy Place and the Holy of Holies.*

*Through reading this book, you will leave with such a revelation and illumination of the myriad facets, functions and features of Him and who you are in Him.*

It's All About Him!

**Bishop Nate Holcomb**
**Bishop & Pastor of the Cathedral of Central Texas Christian House of Prayer and Covenant Connection International.**

---

*God's Blueprint for Spiritual Growth & Reward: The Mosaic Tabernacle is perhaps one of the greatest teaching tools and personal life studies on the Mosaic Tabernacle. Pastor Steve Morgan brings undeniable understanding of God's process to restore humanity through his son, Jesus Christ. It is helpful and profound in its depth and clarity. If you are looking for a foundational and fundamental teaching, this book is a must for all leaders and students of the Bible.*

**Pastor Alvin Smith**
**Son Light Covenant Church**
**Crestview, FL**

# TABLE OF CONTENTS

# LIST OF ILLUSTRATIONS

# ACKNOWLEDGEMENTS

*I give my eternal gratitude to my Lord Jesus Christ who is my all in all and has charged me to write this book. Thanks to my wife Georgette, who teaches me what mature humility looks like; I Love you with all my heart. My daughter Kiliea and son Michael Jr., you both are an inspiration to me; "Much Love!" To Reverend B. R. Hicks, thank you for your teachings, for without them this book would not have been possible... I appreciate you more than you know. Thank you Bishop and Pastor Holcomb for your insight, wisdom, understanding and patience; Thanks for being there when my father passed. Thank you Bishop and Pastor McMillan for your friendship, encouragement and love. For all the Covenant Connections International (CCI) members who encouraged me to move forward on this book, thanks a million! Prophet/Pastor Alvin Smith, you have blessed me immeasurably ...Thank You!*

**To all those who helped me perfect this work:** *Thanks Pastor Neil & Marlene Cassata; Love Ya! My sister, Candi, was instrumental in the cover of this book, how can I express in a few short words how much I love you except, Cha Ching Ching! Tish Davies, thank you for being available. Kyrie Ford, you're a diamond just now being revealed. Erica Eason, I'm honored that you would willingly step in, Thank You!*

# INTRODUCTION

God has been in the reconciling business ever since Adam and Eve took a bite of the fruit from the tree of knowledge of good and evil. The law of **sin and death** took effect and the law of **life in the blood** was the antidote. The blood of the animals God used to provide Adam and Eve coats of skins was used as atonement for their sins that God and man could still commune together. This principle of reconciliation was no secret to Adam and Eve and their offspring. Is it any wonder why God rejected Cain's offering of fruit of the ground and accepted Abel's blood sacrifice? Could Cain have deliberately ignored this principle to try to dictate his relationship with God?

If we allow God to dictate our relationship with Him, then we must study His past, present and future provisions provided to maintain the relationship. We will find that as we study these provisions, we will see that the principles, though they have changed forms, are still the same as was in Israel's journey from Egypt to Canaan's Land, the High Priest's journey from the courtyard to the Holy of Holies in the Mosaic Tabernacle and the Christian's walk from being a babe in Christ to the measure and stature of the fullness of Jesus Christ.

The tabernacle is filled with pictures and glimpses of many facets of Jesus Christ and His nature. Because of the broad connection of the Old and New Testament, this book starts with a general overview and focuses in on some details. Throughout this study, I have approached this work with a picture within a picture mentality. Meaning, if a principle is applicable for a group of people, it is also applicable to an individual.

It should become evident in this book that if God went through so much detail for a tabernacle that could not purge the conscience, then the complete details of Jesus Christ, our more perfect tabernacle, is unfathomable. Furthermore, if these details were important to be accomplished so that mankind could have a relationship with God, then we must mean something greater to God than we realize.

The purpose of this book is to reveal Jesus Christ to you in a way that you have never seen before. Not because of my knowledge base, but because of the limitless One, the Lord Jesus Christ. It's all about Him!

The tabernacle holds a greater number of revelations than could be relayed in this book. Daily I discover a new treasure of truth in this study. Jesus Christ is deeper than any depths that we could achieve in this lifetime. I pray that this book will aid you in your walk with Jesus Christ by helping you discover more about Him.

All scripture references are from the King James Version Bible 1769 unless otherwise noted.

If you, the reader, have any suggestions for improving the next print, please feel free to contact me. My information is located on the last page.

To know Him is to love Him!

Pastor Steve Morgan

# 1

# WHY IS THE TABERNACLE IMPORTANT?

### IT'S ALL ABOUT JESUS!

The complete Bible is all about Jesus. Jesus is the word. It should be no surprise to find that the tabernacle set the stage for His grand appearance and return. The Old Testament and mosaic tabernacle is Jesus Christ concealed while the New Testament is Jesus Christ revealed.

### GOD MENTIONED THE CONSTRUCTION OF THE TABERNACLE 4 TIMES IN THE WORD OF GOD.

Exodus 25:10 – 27:21(God's Instructions on how to build it);
Exodus 37:1 – 38:31 (Obedience to God's Instructions);
Exodus 40:1 – 40:15 (God's Instructs on placement of furniture);
Exodus 40:16 – 40:38 (Obedience to God's Instructions).

The importance of the tabernacle was sufficient for God to walk Moses and all who were involved carefully through the process. Rarely has God allowed anything to be recorded in the Bible four times.

## A MAJORITY OF THE OLD AND NEW TESTAMENT IS CONNECTED TO THE TABERNACLE.

Some scripture is hidden behind a revelation of the tabernacle while others give a direct inference. If the mosaic tabernacle was connected to just 25% of the bible it would behoove us to study this subject. However, God has placed a higher percentage connected to the Mosaic Tabernacle. As we go through this book, we will see that a greater percentage of the bible relates to the tabernacle.

Hebrews 9 reveals that the tabernacle is a figure of Jesus. The depth of our Lord is so great that even a figure of Him has mind blowing revelations.

## GOD SHOWED MOSES THE TABERNACLE IN HEAVEN TO BE DUPLICATED AND PLACED ON EARTH.

**Exodus 25:40** *And look that thou make them after their pattern, which was* <u>*shewed*</u> *thee in the mount.*

The Hebrew word for Shewed is רָאָה, ra'ah, (*raw-aw'*), which means to see, look at, inspect, perceive, consider, learn about, observe and watch.

If the tabernacle was important enough for God to roll back the clouds and show Moses the tabernacle in heaven so that he could build one on earth, there must be some great revelations hidden for the diligent.

So we as Christians should be raw-aw'ing Christ continually. The more ways we see Christ in the word, the easier it is for us to build and walk through the tabernacle in our hearts.

## WE ARE HIGH PRIESTS AND SHOULD KNOW HOW TO MINISTER IN OUR TABERNACLE.

**1 Peter 2:9** *But ye are a chosen generation, a **royal priesthood**, an holy nation, a peculiar people; that ye should shew forth the praises of Him who hath called you out of darkness into his marvelous light:*
**1 Corinthians 3:16** *¶ Know ye not that ye are the temple of God, and that*

*the Spirit of God dwelleth in you?*

As a royal priesthood, we should know how to minister in the temple (tabernacle) in our hearts to aid in our relationship with Jesus. How many times do we allow our temple to be defiled out of ignorance? Ignorance in the ways of God is a dangerous matter.

**Hosea 4:6** ¶ *My people are destroyed for lack of knowledge: because thou hast rejected knowledge, I will also reject thee, that thou shalt be no priest to me: seeing thou hast forgotten the law of thy God, I will also forget thy children.*

Hosea was a prophet who lived during the fall of Israel. Among many sins, they had become passive concerning the principles that God had laid out for them in the law. We don't have to become passive in ministering in the things of God. Let us learn from Hosea's prophecy and continue as priests to God.

### JESUS CAME NOT TO DESTROY THE LAW, BUT TO FULFILL IT.

**Matthew 5:17** ¶ *Think not that I am come to destroy the law, or the prophets: I am not come to destroy, but to fulfill.*

Jesus meticulously fulfilled every law from the Old Testament. Only God could accomplish such precision. Studying the tabernacle will increase your faith as you discover some of the details that Jesus fulfilled. If He can fulfill all the details required for Him to become the final perfect sacrifice to cleanse our conscience, He surely can provide a new life for us.

Time and time again I hear how Jesus saves people by moving so many details in their lives that you can hear their sense of awe as they testify. Let's face it, God is a detailed God! Awesome is a better word!

### JESUS IS OUR HIGH PRIEST AND MEDIATOR, WHO MINISTERS IN THE TABERNACLE IN HEAVEN FOR US.

**Hebrews 9:11** *But Christ being come an high priest of good things to* *come, by a greater and more perfect tabernacle, not made with hands, that is to say, not of this building;*

The mosaic tabernacle gives us a concise picture of the ministry Jesus is performing for us in heaven before the Father. The priest was to minister daily for the people and so Jesus ministers before God for us. How does Jesus walk through the tabernacle as he approaches God? What is the purpose when Jesus stops at a specific piece of furniture in the tabernacle of heaven? Jesus has fulfilled the law and he is our high priest in heaven, we can study the actions of the priests and high priests as they ministered in the mosaic tabernacle to see what our Lord is doing for us right now.

### THE TABERNACLE WAS A FIGURE OR SHADOW OF JESUS CHRIST.

*Hebrews 9:8* ¶ *The Holy Ghost this signifying, that the way into the holiest of all was not yet made manifest, while as the first tabernacle was yet standing:* **9 Which was a figure** *for the time then present, in which were offered both gifts and sacrifices, that could not make him that did the service perfect, as pertaining to the conscience;*

In studying the figure of Jesus, we can find wonderful truths about our Lord, we can understand more of His nature, and we can find a deeper meaning in His actions in the New Testament. In our search for more of Jesus, we will find wonders of His Love in His very figures and shadows.

### WE GET A CLEARER UNDERSTANDING OF SCRIPTURE ONCE WE UNDERSTAND THE TABERNACLE.

With the tabernacle in heaven still intact, we can see revelations in the word of God as we apply the principles set forth in the Mosaic Tabernacle. Applying these principles will help us conclude that the unity of the Old and New Testament substantiates that Jesus is the same yesterday, today and forever. It's comforting to know that God is consistent!

# 2

# *THE MOSAIC TABERNACLE*

Jesus is our more perfect tabernacle because of the things he suffered to fulfill the requirements of the Mosaic Tabernacle. Therefore the Mosaic Tabernacle is an extraordinary picture of Jesus and His nature. As we study the tabernacle, I pray that the Holy Ghost reveal to you a greater understanding of who Jesus is, His perfect fulfillment of the law, and His desire to touch your life miraculously.

The word Tabernacle is translated from the Hebrew word משכן mishkan (*mish-kawn'*) *and means* dwelling, habitation, dwelling place, and tent. There was one tabernacle on earth and still is one in heaven.

## *THE TABERNACLE WAS A COMPASS AND A CROSS.*

### *Compass*

With the use of a compass we can place the tabernacle as God instructed Moses to orient it as it would be arranged when the cloud and fire rested, thus signifying the place where the Israelites would set up the tabernacle and encamp around it.

Just as God started with the Ark of Covenant and the Mercy Seat, we must also start there to orient the tabernacle properly.

*Leviticus 16:14   And he shall take of the blood of the bullock, and sprinkle it with his finger upon the mercy seat eastward; and before the mercy seat shall he sprinkle of the blood with his finger seven times.*

When the High Priest went into the Holy of Holies, Leviticus 16:14 directs him to apply blood only on the east side of the Ark of the Covenant and Mercy Seat. This places the Ark and Mercy Seat west of the High Priest after passing under the veil. With the Ark and Mercy Seat placed in the west, the remaining pieces of furniture would be east of the Ark and Mercy Seat. Exodus 40 tells us that the Golden Table of Shewbread is placed in the North and the Golden Candlestick is located in the South of the Holy Place. Our compass is achieved since the seven pieces of furniture were placed in the form of a cross. (See Figure 1)

It shouldn't surprise the Christian that the cross is our compass through life and to guide us in our relationship with Jesus. Even today the Mosaic tabernacle has some guidance to give to those who pursue a closer walk with Him.

### The Cross

Exodus 40 gives a synopsis of God instructing Moses on the placement of the furniture and Moses' obedience to God's instruction. The seven pieces of furniture were placed in the form of a cross to point the priests to the more perfect tabernacle, Jesus Christ. It was paramount that Jesus be hung on the cross for him to fulfill the law and the tabernacle that prophesied His ultimate sacrifice (See Figure 2).

God gave the instructions concerning the tabernacle from His position down to the position of man. Hence the reason for Him starting at the Ark and Mercy Seat and moving to the Brazen Altar. Man, in order to approach God, started at the Brazin Altar and worked up to the Ark and Mercy Seat. This order sets a precedent to which we should take heed if we are to be successful on our ascension to the Holy of Holies of the Tabernacle in our heart.

Let's take a look at Exodus 40 and see how the tabernacle was laid out.

Mercy Seat

Ark of Covenant

Golden
Candlestick

Golden Alter
of Incense

Golden Table
of Shewbread

Brazin Laver

Brazin Altar

**Figure 1. The Tabernacle as a Compass.**

**The Ark and Mercy Seat.**

God Spoke;
*Exodus 40:1 ¶ And the LORD spake unto Moses, saying, 2 On the first day of the first month shalt thou set up the tabernacle of the tent of the congregation. 3 And thou shalt put therein the ark of the testimony,*

Moses Obeyed;
*Verse 20 And he took and put the testimony into the ark, and set the staves on the ark, and put the mercy seat above upon the ark: 21 And he brought the ark into the tabernacle, and set up the vail of the covering, and covered the ark of the testimony; as the LORD commanded Moses.*

**The Table of Shewbread.**

God Spoke;
*Exodus 40:4a And thou shalt bring in the table, and set in order the things that are to be set in order upon it;*

Moses Obeyed;
*Verse 22 And he put the table in the tent of the congregation, upon the side of the tabernacle **northward**, without the vail. 23 And he set the bread in order upon it before the LORD; as the LORD had commanded Moses.* (See Figure 1)

**The Golden Candlestick.**

God Spoke;
*Exodus 40:4b and thou shalt bring in the candlestick, and light the lamps thereof.*

Moses Obeyed;
*Verse 24 And he put the candlestick in the tent of the congregation, over against the table, on the side of the tabernacle **southward**. 25 And he lighted the lamps before the LORD; as the LORD commanded Moses.* (See Figure 1)

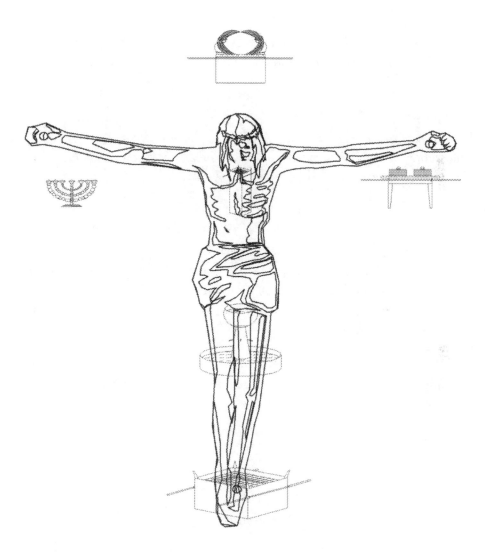

**Figure 2. Mosaic Tabernacle in the Form of a Cross.**

**The Golden Altar of Incense.**

God Spoke;
*Exodus 40: 5 And thou shalt set the altar of gold for the incense before the ark of the testimony, and put the hanging of the door to the tabernacle.*

Moses Obeyed;
*Verse 26 And he put the golden altar in the tent of the congregation before the vail: 27 And he burnt sweet incense thereon; as the LORD commanded Moses.* (See Figure 1)

**The Brazen Altar.**

God Spoke;
*Exodus 40: 6 And thou shalt set the altar of the burnt offering before the door of the tabernacle of the tent of the congregation.*

Moses Obeyed;
*Verse 29 And he put the altar of burnt offering by the door of the tabernacle of the tent of the congregation, and offered upon it the burnt offering and the meat offering; as the LORD commanded Moses.* (See Figure 1)

**The Brazen Laver.**

God Spoke;
*Exodus 40:7 And thou shalt set the Laver between the tent of the congregation and the altar, and shalt put water therein.*

Moses Obeyed;
*Verse 30 And he set the Laver between the tent of the congregation and the altar, and put water there, to wash withal. (See Figure 1)*

Seven is the number of perfection. Notice that God started from where he is (The Ark of the Covenant and Mercy Seat) and proceeded to where man is (The Brazen Altar) through the seven pieces of furniture. If God hadn't approached us first we would not have been able to approach Him. This is consistent with God's plan for reconciliation in that he would send His son from where he was to man.

Now that the way to God had been established, man would be required to approach from the east, through the gate and towards the west. When Adam and Eve were put out of the Garden of Eden they were driven out on the east side. Now man must go west to approach God and to return to that relationship that was in the Garden. This is symbolic of the principle requiring one who leaves God must return to Him the same way he left by dealing with the same issues that they left behind. When God points out an issue that we need to confront and we choose not to submit to His leading, we stop our spiritual growth and place a wedge between God and ourselves. Once we return to the issue that we ignored, our spiritual growth begins again and the wedge is removed. Go west!

**The Gate, Door and Veil.**

The journey to the presence of God meant that the gate, the door, and the veil had to be passed. (See Figure 3)

### The Gate
The Tabernacle was surrounded by a fence of fine linen supported by poles, silver sockets and cordage. When the people of Israel wanted to approach God, they would enter through the gate on the east side of the tabernacle to find themselves in the courtyard.

### The Door
Once entering into the courtyard, a **Blood** sacrifice was offered at the Brazin Laver. Leviticus tells us that supernatural **Fire** from God would consume the sacrifice; signifying that the offering was acceptable. The priests would then wash their hands and feet with **Water** from the Brazin Altar.

*Heb 9:22 And almost all things are by the law purged with blood; and without shedding of blood is no remission.*

With the purging power of blood, fire and water completed, the priests would walk through the door of the tabernacle into the Holy Place.

The Holy Place was the second third of the tabernacle. Here the Golden Altar of Incense was the first order of business. The incense represented prayer and the priests were to tend to prayer every time they approached the Golden Altar of prayer. From there the priests would move to the Golden Candlestick and add oil and fire that produced light for them to minister by. After the Golden Candlestick ministry, the priests would approach the Golden Altar of Prayer and offer more prayer. Then they would approach the Golden Table of Shewbread where they would set in order the frankincense (signifying Faith) and eat of the Shewbread. The priests would then return to the Altar of Prayer and exit the Holy Place through the door into the Courtyard.

### The Veil

Once a year the High Priest would approach the Holy of Holies the same way the Priests would minister except upon the third time approaching the Golden Altar of Prayer, he would crawl under the veil with blood and incense to approach the Ark of Covenant and Mercy Seat where the Lord said he would sit between the cherubim.

Jesus said that he came to fulfill the law:

*Mt 5:17 ¶ Think not that I am come to destroy the law, or the prophets: I am not come to destroy, but to fulfill.*

With Jesus fulfilling the Tabernacle, he became the more perfect Tabernacle.

*Heb 9:11 But Christ being come an high priest of good things to come, by a greater and more perfect tabernacle, not made with hands, that is to say, not of this building;*

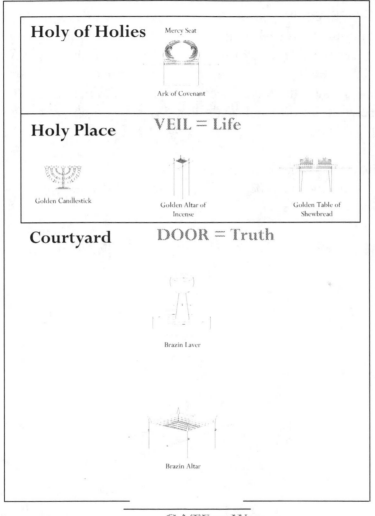

Figure 3. The Mosaic Tabernacle.

***John 14:6*** *Jesus saith unto him, I am the way, the truth, and the life: no man cometh unto the Father, but by me.*

Jesus fulfilled the gate by being the way into salvation, the door by being the truth that reveals to us who we are and the veil by being the life that only Jesus can give. When we ask Jesus into our hearts, we have entered into the way. As we face the truth of ourselves and the word of God we enter into the truth. Once we've passed through the truth, we can then receive life more abundantly that Jesus spoke about as we let this mind of Christ be in us.

***John 10:10*** *The thief cometh not, but for to steal, and to kill, and to destroy: I am come that they might have life, and that they might have [it] more abundantly.*

It is Jesus' desire that all grow into this life more abundantly.

# 3

## ISRAEL'S JOURNEY

### (FROM EGYPT TO CANAAN'S LAND)

Before we continue with the Mosaic Tabernacle, we need to go over Israel's Journey from Egypt to Canaan's Land to see some patterns that will be repeated in the Mosaic Tabernacle and in today's Christian walk. Through God's perfect consistency, he has laid out a road map for His followers to cultivate a maturing relationship with Him. Hebrews 13:8 best summarizes this:

**Hebrews 13:8** *Jesus Christ the same yesterday, and today, and forever.*

Knowing that Jesus is the same in the past, present and future enables us to derive certain principles from the scriptures that will never fail us.

Israel's Journey from Egypt to Canaan's Land, The Mosaic Tabernacle and the Christian's pattern for growth are parallel in principle. These principles established in the Old Testament are fulfilled by Jesus Christ and laid out for the Christian to grow to the measure and stature of Jesus Christ so that this is that which was done by God in the Old Testament and fulfilled by JESUS in the New Testament.

There were three major divisions in Israel's journey to the Promise Land: I Deliverance from Egypt, II the Wilderness of Testing and Trials and III Canaan's Land.

The Tabernacle also had three major divisions: The Courtyard, The Holy Place and The Holy of Holies.

As Christians, we experience three major divisions in our journey: Redemption from Sin, Testing and Trials and Maturity to the Measure and Stature of Jesus Christ. Let's take a look at Israel's journey and see the similarity to a Christian's walk into maturity.

The first third of Israel's journey started with the deliverance from slavery in Egypt. They were led to and across the Red Sea by the pillar of cloud by day and fire by night as a free people.

The wilderness was simply the second third of their journey and it was never God's intention to take forty years to get to the next stage. The wilderness of testing and trials was designed to show Israel what was in their heart and the tabernacle was designed to cleanse Israel of their unbelief. Through the wilderness, the younger generation learned to trust the Lord and see His sovereignty to prepare them for the final third of their trip to Canaan's Land.

Canaan's Land is also known as Beulah Land or Marriage Land, and is a place that requires maturity. With the current divorce rate, we know that marriage is not for children. In Canaan's land, the Israelites needed to accomplish three things; 1. Take the Land, 2. Divide the Land, 3. Keep the land.

Let's take a closer look at the Deliverance, Wilderness and Canaan's Land experiences.

## (I.) Deliverance from Egypt; the Blood, Fire and Water

The Israelites were completely set free from their hard task masters only after they had gone through the Blood, Fire, and Water experience. Although the Egyptians had let them go under the blood, Israel's liberty was short lived because Pharaoh went to recapture his slaves and was held at bay by the Pillar of Cloud and Fire until the Red Sea was parted and the Israelites were safely across. Once the Pillar of Cloud released Pharaoh and his army, they pursued the Israelites into the Red Sea where God destroyed them with water. Israel had the pleasure of seeing God destroy their enemy as they began their journey in the wilderness.

When you read Exodus Chapter 1 – 11, you will find that before Israel could enter into the wilderness, they were delivered by the **Blood**, led and protected by the Pillar of Cloud by day and **Fire** by night, and baptized through the Red Sea (**Water**) (See Figure 4). These three elements not only prepared them for the next stage of their journey, it separated them from the enemy and bondage completely. The blood, fire, and water experience was intended for judgment and separation.

### Blood

*Exodus 12:12  For I will pass through the land of Egypt this night, and will smite all the firstborn in the land of Egypt, both man and beast; and against all the gods of Egypt I will execute judgment: I am the LORD. 13 And the blood shall be to you for a token upon the houses where ye are: and when I see the blood, I will pass over you, and the plague shall not be upon you to destroy you, when I smite the land of Egypt.*

Israel's separation started with the last of the ten plagues God brought to Egypt by Moses. God told Israel to take a first year male lamb without spot or blemish and kill the lamb for Passover. The blood was to be placed on the two side posts and the upper door post (lintel) which formed a blood cross. As they were instructed to eat the Passover, Exodus 12:46 reveals that they were not to break any bones of the lamb. When the judgment of God passed over a house marked with a blood cross, the household was spared the judgment against the first born. The blood was then used as a mark for the Egyptians to cast the people out of their presence.

### Fire

*Exodus 13: 21  And the LORD went before them by day in a pillar of a cloud, to lead them the way; and by night in a pillar of fire, to give them light; to go by day and night: 22 He took not away the pillar of the cloud by day, nor the pillar of fire by night, from before the people.*

After Egypt exiled all those who had the blood cross on their doors, God provided a leader and guide for Israel to go before them as they journeyed in the form of a pillar of cloud by day and pillar of fire by night. Not only did the pillar of cloud and fire lead the people through their journey, but the cloud was present during the day to provide protection from the hot desert sun while the fire was present during the cooler nights to light and warm God's people. It was also a great darkness to the enemies of God.

When Israel was at the shore of the Red sea, the pillar of cloud and fire was placed between the enemy of God and His people. This pillar was simultaneously a cloud of darkness to God's enemies and light to His sons and daughters.

*Exodus 14:10 ¶ And when Pharaoh drew nigh, the children of Israel lifted up their eyes, and, behold, the Egyptians marched after them; and they were sore afraid: and the children of Israel cried out unto the LORD. 13 And Moses said unto the people, Fear ye not, stand still, and see the salvation of the LORD, which he will shew to you today: for the Egyptians whom ye have seen today, ye shall see them again no more forever. 14 The LORD shall fight for you, and ye shall hold your peace. 19 And the angel of God, which went before the camp of Israel, removed and went behind them; and the pillar of the cloud went from before their face, and stood behind them: 20 And it came between the camp of the Egyptians and the camp of Israel; and it was a cloud and darkness [to them], but it gave light by night [to these]: so that the one came not near the other all the night.*

### Water

The blood separated them from the lifestyle of sin. The fire led and guided them and separated them from the Egyptians who wanted to take their slaves back. Finally, the water destroyed the pursing armies and severed all strings to the former lifestyle. I am convinced that had the Israelites not followed the pillar of cloud by day and fire by night and crossed the Red Sea that their pursuers would have overtaken them to destroy or bring them back into bondage. This holds true for both the new and mature Christian. We must follow the leading and guidance of the Holy Ghost for he will lead us into increasing liberty in Christ.

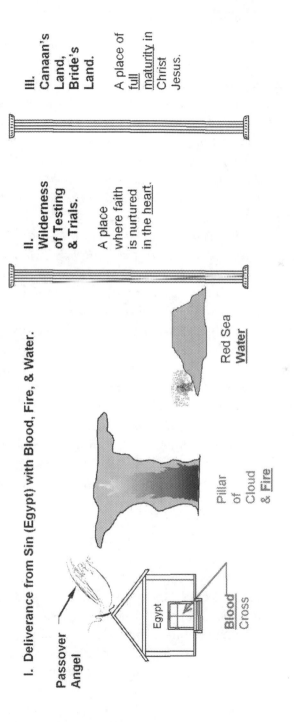

I. Deliverance from Sin (Egypt) with Blood, Fire, & Water.

Passover Angel

Egypt

Blood
Cross

Pillar
of
Cloud
& Fire

Red Sea
Water

II.
Wilderness
of Testing
& Trials.

A place
where faith
is nurtured
in the heart.

III.
Canaan's
Land,
Bride's
Land.

A place of
full
maturity in
Christ
Jesus.

Figure 4. Israel's Journey to Canaan's Land

19

*Exodus 14:21* ¶ *And Moses stretched out his hand over the sea; and the LORD caused the sea to go [back] by a strong east wind all that night, and made the sea dry [land], and the waters were divided. 22 And the children of Israel went into the midst of the sea upon the dry [ground]: and the waters [were] a wall unto them on their right hand, and on their left. 23 And the Egyptians pursued, and went in after them to the midst of the sea, [even] all Pharaoh's horses, his chariots, and his horsemen. 24 And it came to pass, that in the morning watch the LORD looked unto the host of the Egyptians through the pillar of fire and of the cloud, and troubled the host of the Egyptians, 25 And took off their chariot wheels, that they drave them heavily: so that the Egyptians said, Let us flee from the face of Israel; for the LORD fighteth for them against the Egyptians. 26 And the LORD said unto Moses, Stretch out thine hand over the sea, that the waters may come again upon the Egyptians, upon their chariots, and upon their horsemen. 27 And Moses stretched forth his hand over the sea, and the sea returned to his strength when the morning appeared; and the Egyptians fled against it; and the LORD overthrew the Egyptians in the midst of the sea. 28 And the waters returned, and covered the chariots, and the horsemen, [and] all the host of Pharaoh that came into the sea after them; there remained not so much as one of them. 29 But the children of Israel walked upon dry [land] in the midst of the sea; and the waters [were] a wall unto them on their right hand, and on their left. 30 Thus the LORD saved Israel that day out of the hand of the Egyptians; and Israel saw the Egyptians dead upon the sea shore.*

God knew that the Egyptians would continue to pursue their slaves unless they were utterly destroyed. Finally, Israel was walking as a free people in freedom and liberty from their captors.

The Blood, Fire and Water experiences were outward demonstrations of God's work on Israel's spiritual maturing process used to separate them from their sinful environment into a more Godly one. The second third of their maturing process (the Wilderness) was primarily focused on matters of the heart both corporately and individually.

## (II.) Wilderness

The wilderness was where the Israelites received the Mosaic Tabernacle and also where God began to show them that they could trust Him for their personal needs. God wanted them to come to Him for their many concerns. The wilderness was initially intended for just a few months but their inability to take in what the Lord had done as a record of what he will do for them caused the Israelites to spend forty years there. Remembering what the Lord has done for us in the past helps to have faith in our current circumstances; I call it "Remembering your Red Sea Card". The wilderness tested the character of Israel and taught them what was in their hearts while God provided a way of repentance and reconciliation.

***Deuteronomy 8:2** And thou shalt remember all the way which the LORD thy God led thee these forty years in the wilderness, to humble thee, [and] to prove thee, to know what [was] in thine heart, whether thou wouldest keep his commandments, or no.*

Let's look at some of the trials that the Israelites experienced in the wilderness. You will probably find that their experiences are not very different from ours as Christians. As a matter of fact, 1 Corinthians 10 shares how their experiences were to show us how to know what to do and what not to do. Looking at the results helps us determine what pleases and displeases God.

***1Co 10:1** ¶ Moreover, brethren, I would not that ye should be ignorant, how that all our fathers were under the cloud, and all passed through the sea; **2** And were all baptized unto Moses in the cloud and in the sea; **3** And did all eat the same spiritual meat; **4** And did all drink the same spiritual drink: for they drank of that spiritual Rock that followed them: and that Rock was Christ. **5** But with many of them God was not well pleased: for they were overthrown in the wilderness. **6** ¶ Now these things were our examples, to the intent we should not lust after evil things, as they also lusted. . .*

### Trial of Murmuring

Although Israel was delivered and set apart for God, they were in great need for development in their thoughts and the way they dealt with their problems. They still had a mentality of a slave even though they saw their master destroyed. Whenever a need arose, they would begin to murmur against God by murmuring against Moses and Aaron. Initially God overlooked their murmuring and let them know that he heard them and gave them what they needed. It would appear obvious that all they had to do was seek God and he would answer and provide. However, their separation from the cruel taskmasters did not change their thinking. Many of us can relate to this. God wanted to develop a relationship such that Israel would trust Him completely.

The Hebrew word for Murmur is לוּן luwn (*loon*) or לִין liyn (*leen*) which means to grumble or complain.

### Murmuring for Water

*Exodus 15:23  And when they came to Marah, they could not drink of the waters of Marah, for they [were] bitter: therefore the name of it was called Marah. 24  And the people murmured against Moses, saying, What shall we drink?  25  And he cried unto the LORD; and the LORD shewed him a tree, [which] when he had cast into the waters, the waters were made sweet: there he made for them a statute and an ordinance, and there he proved them,  26  And said, If thou wilt diligently hearken to the voice of the LORD thy God, and wilt do that which is right in his sight, and wilt give ear to his commandments, and keep all his statutes, I will put none of these diseases upon thee, which I have brought upon the Egyptians: for I [am] the LORD that healeth thee.*

The first place the Israelites came to after the Red Sea was Marah. God showed great mercy to allow them to receive the revelation that they didn't have to approach God like they were slaves or disgruntled workers as they did in Egypt. Had they remembered collectively that the Lord destroyed their enemies with the Red Sea; maybe they could have taken confidence that He could provide food and water as well.

## Murmuring for Food

*Exodus 16:2   And the whole congregation of the children of Israel murmured against Moses and Aaron in the wilderness:   3   And the children of Israel said unto them, Would to God we had died by the hand of the LORD in the land of Egypt, when we sat by the flesh pots, and when we did eat bread to the full; for ye have brought us forth into this wilderness, to kill this whole assembly with hunger.   6   And Moses and Aaron said unto all the children of Israel, At even, then ye shall know that the LORD hath brought you out from the land of Egypt:   7   And in the morning, then ye shall see the glory of the LORD; for that he heareth your murmurings against the LORD: and what are we, that ye murmur against us?   8   And Moses said, This shall be, when the LORD shall give you in the evening flesh to eat, and in the morning bread to the full; for that the LORD heareth your murmurings which ye murmur against him: and what are we? your murmurings are not against us, but against the LORD.   9   And Moses spake unto Aaron, Say unto all the congregation of the children of Israel, Come near before the LORD: for he hath heard your murmurings.   10   And it came to pass, as Aaron spake unto the whole congregation of the children of Israel, that they looked toward the wilderness, and, behold, the glory of the LORD appeared in the cloud.   11   And the LORD spake unto Moses, saying,   12   I have heard the murmurings of the children of Israel: speak unto them, saying, At even ye shall eat flesh, and in the morning ye shall be filled with bread; and ye shall know that I am the LORD your God.   13 ¶ And it came to pass, that at even the quails came up, and covered the camp: and in the morning the dew lay round about the host.   14   And when the dew that lay was gone up, behold, upon the face of the wilderness there lay a small round thing, as small as the hoar frost on the ground.   15   And when the children of Israel saw it, they said one to another, It is manna: for they wist not what it was. And Moses said unto them, This is the bread which the LORD hath given you to eat.*

At this point in their development, another lesson was added in that when they murmured against the leaders God had set before them, they were actually murmuring against the Lord. Israel was being taught principles to help them stay out of trouble with God. Many times we as

Christians are careless to murmur against our pastor and/or leadership. This type of slave mentality can keep us from growing beyond our own limitations.

**Exodus 16:35** *And the children of Israel did eat manna forty years, until they came to a land inhabited; they did eat manna, until they came unto the borders of the land of Canaan.*

### The Second Murmuring for Water

**Exodus 17:1** ¶ *And all the congregation of the children of Israel journeyed from the wilderness of Sin, after their journeys, according to the commandment of the LORD, and pitched in Rephidim: and there was no water for the people to drink. 2 Wherefore the people did chide with Moses, and said, Give us water that we may drink. And Moses said unto them, Why chide ye with me? wherefore do ye tempt the LORD? 3 And the people thirsted there for water; and the people murmured against Moses, and said, Wherefore is this that thou hast brought us up out of Egypt, to kill us and our children and our cattle with thirst? 4 And Moses cried unto the LORD, saying, What shall I do unto this people? they be almost ready to stone me. 5 And the LORD said unto Moses, Go on before the people, and take with thee of the elders of Israel; and thy rod, wherewith thou smotest the river, take in thine hand, and go. 6 Behold, I will stand before thee there upon the rock in Horeb; and thou shalt smite the rock, and there shall come water out of it, that the people may drink. And Moses did so in the sight of the elders of Israel. 7 And he called the name of the place Massah, and Meribah, because of the chiding of the children of Israel, and because they tempted the LORD, saying, Is the LORD among us, or not?*

In this connotation the Hebrew word for Chide is רִיב riyb *reeb* or רוּב ruwb *roob* which means to strive, contend, chide, debate, physically, to conduct a case or suit (legal), sue, to make complaint, and to quarrel.

It seems that the people were becoming more adamant about their needs and less concerned about sinning against God. Their need for water was legitimate and needed to be addressed. However, the way they sought to fulfill their need was sinful. I believe that God would have brought water from a rock if they had fallen on their face before Him and humbly asked Him for water. Their lack of trust in God's system of provisions was displayed by the way they went about it.

Before we cast any stones, I would like to point out that in our walk, we have done the same thing. Instead of seeking God for His intervention, we set out to solve problems by our own wisdom and cunning. How much more could we have benefited if we would have let God lead us through the process?

### Trial of War

This was the first battle Israel faced as a free people. Among countless lessons here, I want to mention that God used the headship to keep the people victorious. Moses was in need of assistance to sustain the victory when Aaron and Hur stepped up to support the work.

*Exodus 17:8 ¶ Then came Amalek, and fought with Israel in Rephidim. 9 And Moses said unto Joshua, Choose us out men, and go out, fight with Amalek: to morrow I will stand on the top of the hill with the rod of God in mine hand. {Joshua: called Jesus} 10 So Joshua did as Moses had said to him, and fought with Amalek: and Moses, Aaron, and Hur went up to the top of the hill. 11 And it came to pass, when Moses held up his hand, that Israel prevailed: and when he let down his hand, Amalek prevailed. 12 But Moses' hands [were] heavy; and they took a stone, and put [it] under him, and he sat thereon; and Aaron and Hur stayed up his hands, the one on the one side, and the other on the other side; and his hands were steady until the going down of the sun. 13 And Joshua discomfited Amalek and his people with the edge of the sword. 14 And the LORD said unto Moses, Write this [for] a memorial in a book, and rehearse [it] in the ears of Joshua: for I will utterly put out the remembrance of Amalek from under heaven. 15 And Moses built an altar, and called the name of it Jehovahnissi: {Jehovahnissi: that is, The LORD my banner} 16 For he said, Because the LORD hath sworn [that] the LORD [will have] war with Amalek from generation to generation.*

What an exhilarating experience it must have been to go from slave to victor in a matter of weeks.

When a Christian experiences his first victory the joy is so wonderful. His testimony is filled with wonder and his faith has been strengthened. It's important that we record the blessings of the Lord by writing them in a journal to recall our past experiences where the Lord has caused us to have victory over our situations.

### The Trial of Restructuring

No sooner than they experienced great victory, God sent Moses' father-in-law to restructure their lives. They saw that Moses was truly their leader and now they had to learn to trust subordinate leadership. Not only was this affecting the people, but Moses had to trust God concerning those who were placed in authority.

*Exodus 18:13 ¶ And it came to pass on the morrow, that Moses sat to judge the people: and the people stood by Moses from the morning unto the evening. 14 And when Moses' father in law saw all that he did to the people, he said, What [is] this thing that thou doest to the people? why sittest thou thyself alone, and all the people stand by thee from morning unto even? 15 And Moses said unto his father in law, Because the people come unto me to enquire of God: 16 When they have a matter, they come unto me; and I judge between one and another, and I do make [them] know the statutes of God, and his laws 17 And Moses' father in law said unto him, The thing that thou doest [is] not good. 18 Thou wilt surely wear away, both thou, and this people that [is] with thee: for this thing [is] too heavy for thee; thou art not able to perform it thyself alone. 19 Hearken now unto my voice, I will give thee counsel, and God shall be with thee: Be thou for the people to God-ward, that thou mayest bring the causes unto God: 20 And thou shalt teach them ordinances and laws, and shalt shew them the way wherein they must walk, and the work that they must do. 21 Moreover thou shalt provide out of all the people able men, such as fear God, men of truth, hating covetousness; and place [such] over them, [to be] rulers of thousands, [and] rulers of hundreds, rulers of fifties, and rulers of tens: 22 And let them judge the people at all seasons: and it shall be, [that] every great matter they shall bring unto thee, but every small matter they shall judge: so shall it be easier for thyself, and they shall bear [the burden] with thee. 23 If thou shalt do* _this thing, and God command thee [so], then thou shalt be able to endure, and all this people shall also go to their place in peace. **24** So Moses hearkened to the voice of his father in law, and did all that he had said. **25** And Moses chose able men out of all Israel, and made them heads over the people, rulers of thousands, rulers of hundreds, rulers of fifties, and rulers of tens. **26** And they judged the people at all seasons: the hard causes they brought unto Moses, but every small matter they judged themselves._

Restructuring is important to a Christian's walk. As we develop into mature saints, we will have restructured our priorities, time, gifts, talents, and possessions many times. Let us embrace this liberating change so that God will draw out all the beauty that lies within us.

Sometimes the enemy will try to convince us that if we pass on the reigns as leaders that the work will fall apart. But God would have us to concentrate on training others to do what we do, and then the work will continue as the leader continues to follow Christ's direction. When a leader trains his successor to do what he does, he enables himself to move on to new challenges without disrupting the work at hand.

### The Experience of Mount Sinai

**Exodus 19:9** ¶ _And the LORD said unto Moses, Lo, I come unto thee in a thick cloud, that the people may hear when I speak with thee, and believe thee for ever. And Moses told the words of the people unto the LORD. **10** And the LORD said unto Moses, Go unto the people, and sanctify them today and tomorrow, and let them wash their clothes, **11** And be ready against the third day: for the third day the LORD will come down in the sight of all the people upon mount Sinai. **12** And thou shalt set bounds unto the people round about, saying, Take heed to yourselves, [that ye] go [not] up into the mount, or touch the border of it: whosoever toucheth the mount shall be surely put to death: **13** There shall not an hand touch it, but he shall surely be stoned, or shot through; whether [it be] beast or man, it shall not live: when the trumpet soundeth long, they shall come up to the mount. **14** And Moses went down from the mount unto the people, and sanctified the people; and they washed their clothes. **15** And he said unto the people, Be ready against the third day: come not_ *at [your] wives. 16 ¶ And it came to pass on the third day in the morning, that there were thunders and lightnings, and a thick cloud upon the mount, and the voice of the trumpet exceeding loud; so that all the people that [was] in the camp trembled. 18 And mount Sinai was altogether on a smoke, because the LORD descended upon it in fire: and the smoke thereof ascended as the smoke of a furnace, and the whole mount quaked greatly. 19 And when the voice of the trumpet sounded long, and waxed louder and louder, Moses spake, and God answered him by a voice. 20 And the LORD came down upon mount Sinai, on the top of the mount: and the LORD called Moses [up] to the top of the mount; and Moses went up. 21 And the LORD said unto Moses, Go down, charge the people, lest they break through unto the LORD to gaze, and many of them perish. 22 And let the priests also, which come near to the LORD, sanctify themselves, lest the LORD break forth upon them. 23 And Moses said unto the LORD, The people cannot come up to mount Sinai: for thou chargedst us, saying, Set bounds about the mount, and sanctify it. 25 So Moses went down unto the people, and spake unto them.*

God wants to establish Himself through a designated voice. He does this by backing the man or woman he has chosen to do his work. Who is your voice of God? Do you take heed to your voice of God?

### The Ten Commandments

God gave the Ten Commandments to help mankind identify their status with Him. With Jesus Christ's sacrifice, we can be redeemed to place our status as sons of God.

***Exodus 20:1** ¶ And God spake all these words, saying, 2 I [am] the LORD thy God, which have brought thee out of the land of Egypt, out of the house of bondage. 3 (**Commandment 1**) Thou shalt have no other gods before me. 4 (**Commandment 2**) Thou shalt not make unto thee any graven image, or any likeness [of anything] that [is] in heaven above, or that [is] in the earth beneath, or that [is] in the water under the earth: 5 Thou shalt not bow down thyself to them, nor serve them: for I the LORD thy God [am] a jealous God, visiting the iniquity of the fathers upon the children unto the third and fourth [generation] of them that hate me; 6 And shewing mercy unto thousands of them that love me, and keep my* *commandments. 7 (Commandment 3) Thou shalt not take the name of the LORD thy God in vain; for the LORD will not hold him guiltless that taketh his name in vain. 8 (Commandment 4) Remember the sabbath day, to keep it holy. 9 Six days shalt thou labour, and do all thy work: 10 But the seventh day [is] the sabbath of the LORD thy God: [in it] thou shalt not do any work, thou, nor thy son, nor thy daughter, thy manservant, nor thy maidservant, nor thy cattle, nor thy stranger that [is] within thy gates: 11 For [in] six days the LORD made heaven and earth, the sea, and all that in them [is], and rested the seventh day: wherefore the LORD blessed the sabbath day, and hallowed it. 12 ¶ (Commandment 5) Honour thy father and thy mother: that thy days may be long upon the land which the LORD thy God giveth thee. 13 (Commandment 6) Thou shalt not kill. 14 (Commandment 7) Thou shalt not commit adultery. 15 (Commandment 8) Thou shalt not steal. 16 (Commandment 9) Thou shalt not bear false witness against thy neighbour. 17 (Commandment 10) Thou shalt not covet thy neighbour's house, thou shalt not covet thy neighbour's wife, nor his manservant, nor his maidservant, nor his ox, nor his ass, nor any thing that [is] thy neighbour's. 18 ¶ And all the people saw the thunderings, and the lightnings, and the noise of the trumpet, and the mountain smoking: and when the people saw [it], they removed, and stood afar off. 19 And they said unto Moses, Speak thou with us, and we will hear: but let not God speak with us, lest we die. 20 And Moses said unto the people, Fear not: for God is come to prove you, and that his fear may be before your faces, that ye sin not. 21 And the people stood afar off, and Moses drew near unto the thick darkness where God [was].*

At Mount Sinai the presence of God was greater than it had ever been to the Israelites. Though they had seen the hand of God move miraculously before, this increased power and the presence of God did not occur until they endured the Blood, Fire, Water experience and entered into the Wilderness. However, to whom much is given, much is required.

Israel was given the Ten Commandments by the voice of God. The people were afraid of the presence of God to the point that they chose Moses' voice over God's. And in that same discourse, Moses revealed one of the purposes God had for showing Himself as he did before the people. Again verse 20 states "And Moses said unto the people, Fear not: for God is come to prove you, and that His fear may be before your faces, that ye sin not."

When we as Christians enter into the wilderness portion of our journey, we will be confronted by the presence of God greater than we have known. Some shrink away, while others understand that an increase in the Lord's presence is an indication of drawing closer to Jesus. Maturity and our proximity to God are synonymous. As we draw closer to Jesus and Him to us, we must trust that His presence before us will do us no harm in those times of increased awareness of God's Glory. The flesh will fear for its life but we must not listen to its council and abide in the glory set before us at that moment. As we continue at the stage of glory in which we find ourselves in, we will grow in confidence at that level. Rest assured that the presence of God is like the trumpet in Exodus 19:19, it waxes greater and greater to no end. Don't be content with the glory and presence of the Lord yesterday provided. Press in and pursue the Lord. Let the fear of God truly cause you to walk in His commandments and judgments.

### Received the Judgments of God

From Exodus 20:22 to chapter 23:19 Israel receives instructions from God on the expected behavior and laws for His people. It was the people who were required to walk in these statutes by their own choice. However, the rewards for choosing to walk accordingly were as significant as the curses from disobedience.

### Received An Angel From The Lord

*Exodus 23:20 ¶ Behold, I send an Angel before thee, to keep thee in the way, and to bring thee into the place which I have prepared. 21 Beware of him, and obey his voice, provoke him not; for he will not pardon your transgressions: for my name is in him. 22 But if thou shalt indeed obey his voice, and do all that I speak; then I will be an enemy unto thine enemies, and an adversary unto thine adversaries. 23 For mine Angel shall go before thee, and bring thee in unto the Amorites, and the Hittites, and the Perizzites, and the Canaanites, the Hivites, and the Jebusites: and*

*I will cut them off. 24 Thou shalt not bow down to their gods, nor serve them, nor do after their works: but thou shalt utterly overthrow them, and quite break down their images. 25 And ye shall serve the LORD your God, and he shall bless thy bread, and thy water; and I will take sickness away from the midst of thee. 26 There shall nothing cast their young, nor be barren, in thy land: the number of thy days I will fulfil. 27 I will send my fear before thee, and will destroy all the people to whom thou shalt come, and I will make all thine enemies turn their backs unto thee. 28 And I will send hornets before thee, which shall drive out the Hivite, the Canaanite, and the Hittite, from before thee. 29 I will not drive them out from before thee in one year; lest the land become desolate, and the beast of the field multiply against thee. 30 By little and little I will drive them out from before thee, until thou be increased, and inherit the land.*

At this point, God began to address His instructions for the final third of their journey, Canaan's Land. God sent an angel before the people to bring them to the Promise Land. In Exodus 20:22 through 23:19 God gave judgments for the people to walk in. If they obeyed these statutes and followed the leading of the angel, their journey would be successful. In obedience, Israel's enemies would be God's enemies and Israel's allies would be God's allies. He promised to go before them in the Promised Land and that they would utterly destroy the enemy. They would be fruitful and the number of their days would be fulfilled. Again, chapter 23 verse 29 & 30 reveal that it would be a process of development and not a sudden deliverance.

When a Christian walks in obedience to the word of God, he receives the same promise as the Israelites. Because this angel has the Lord's name in Him, He will not contradict the word of God. This obedience to the angel and the word of God isn't driven by a feeling, rather an understanding that the word is the only guideline that can produce effective results. The New Testament church has the leader and guider to all truth which is the Holy Ghost as their angel. The Holy Ghost not only has the name of God on Him, He is part of the Triune Godhead. Therefore, he will lead us in greater dimensions than the angel over Israel could. Let us not provoke the angel or Holy Ghost set before us by being obedient to His leading and the word of God so that we will succeed in our journey.

### The Promise of the Promised Land

***Exodus 23:31*** *And I will set thy bounds from the Red sea even unto the sea of the Philistines, and from the desert unto the river: for I will deliver the inhabitants of the land into your hand; and thou shalt drive them out before thee. **32** Thou shalt make no covenant with them, nor with their gods. **33** They shall not dwell in thy land, lest they make thee sin against me: for if thou serve their gods, it will surely be a snare unto thee.*

This is the will of God to allow Israel to possess all the Land without compromise. No covenant was to be made with any of the inhabitants. They were not to cohabitate with the enemy because this would cause them to sin against God by serving other gods. A byproduct of entering a covenant with the Canaanites would cause their inheritance to be reduced.

### *Israel's Vow to Be Obedient*

***Exodus 24:1*** *¶ And he said unto Moses, Come up unto the LORD, thou, and Aaron, Nadab, and Abihu, and seventy of the elders of Israel; and worship ye afar off. **2** And Moses alone shall come near the LORD: but they shall not come nigh; neither shall the people go up with him. **3** And Moses came and told the people all the words of the LORD, and all the judgments:* **and all the people answered with one voice, and said, All the words which the LORD hath said will we do.** *4 And Moses wrote all the words of the LORD, and rose up early in the morning, and builded an altar under the hill, and twelve pillars, according to the twelve tribes of Israel. **5** And he sent young men of the children of Israel, which offered burnt offerings, and sacrificed peace offerings of oxen unto the LORD. **6** And Moses took half of the blood, and put it in basons; and half of the blood he sprinkled on the altar. **7** And he took the book of the covenant, and read in the audience of the people:* **and they said, All that the LORD hath said will we do, and be obedient.** *8 And Moses took the blood, and sprinkled it on the people, and said, Behold the blood of the covenant, which the LORD hath made with you concerning all these words.*

A blood covenant is the most serious of all covenants and was not to be taken lightly; we'll cover the blood covenant later. God will hold all who enter such a high contract responsible for keeping their commitment. God will keep His share of the promise if we keep ours. However, He is not obligated to perform His promise if we default on ours.

It is a rewarding experience to enter into a blood covenant with God through Jesus Christ and walk therein. Many view promises to God as restricting and a sure way to curse oneself. The truth is that a blood covenant is very liberating and enables many to find themselves blessed beyond imagination. The final question still remains: Will you do all that the Lord has said and be obedient?

### The Test of Waiting on God

Exodus 24:9 to 33:17 shares how Moses went up to Mount Sinai. After forty days and nights, Israel grew impatient and gathered to do something about their situation. They made a golden calf from the earrings broken out of the people's ears. I find it interesting that, when their patience for waiting on God to give them the next step waned, they sinned by breaking the first commandment given to them earlier. They mistook waiting on God as doing nothing; thereby they reasoned that they must do something, even if it contradicted the commandment.

Waiting on God is a very proactive stance. It is anything but doing nothing. After I received confirmation through a prophet that I was to be a preacher, I entered a blood covenant with the Lord that I would keep my calling in my heart until my headship recognized it first. Sixteen years later my pastor approached me concerning my call and was ordained as an exhorter and two years later a minister. I remember the times of studying and praying and waiting. There were times I felt I would just burst! However, I kept my vow and I'm so glad that I did. As Christians we will have to learn to wait on God for many things and the benefits are enumerable.

### The Second Test of Waiting on God

Exodus 33:18 to 34:35 shows Moses retuning to Mount Sinai for forty days and nights. Here the Lord gave the Ten Commandments on stone again and further instructions on how to conduct themselves in the final third of their journey. Notice that the Word does not record that the people failed a second time.

I believe that if they had passed the test the first time, they would not have had to return to this trial. When God is developing a nation or a person, the test before them must be passed before they can go any further. If we find we keep going through the same things, then it's time to seek the Lord about responding differently to the test that would allow us to move forward.

### The Possession Trial

*Exodus 35: 4  And Moses spake unto all the congregation of the children of Israel, saying, This is the thing which the LORD commanded, saying, 5 Take ye from among you an offering unto the LORD: whosoever is of a willing heart, let him bring it, an offering of the LORD; gold, and silver, and brass, 6  And blue, and purple, and scarlet, and fine linen, and goats' hair, 7  And rams' skins dyed red, and badgers' skins, and shittim wood, 8 And oil for the light, and spices for anointing oil, and for the sweet incense, 9  And onyx stones, and stones to be set for the ephod, and for the breastplate.*

*Exodus 36: 6 And Moses gave commandment, and they caused it to be proclaimed throughout the camp, saying, Let neither man nor woman make any more work for the offering of the sanctuary. So the people were restrained from bringing. 7 For the stuff they had was sufficient for all the work to make it, and too much.*

One of the early trials in the wilderness God tested them with was their money and possessions. Their trust in God would be demonstrated by their giving from a willing heart. God clearly stipulated that only those with a willing heart could give. From Exodus 36:6 you see that they were willing to give in abundance because of the gratitude they had for the forgiveness they had just received concerning the golden calf.

Many of us are moved by the forgiveness the Lord has bestowed upon us and we give our tithes, we give our offerings and we plant our seeds with a willing heart to provide for His house. Nothing moves God more than an attitude of gratitude.

**The Task of Building the Tabernacle**

From Exodus 36: 8 to the end of the book, God gives instructions concerning the building of the tabernacle. Many had a part in the work of the Lord. One man could not have finished the work. It's common for the Lord's work to require many hands. The Lord causes this to be so for many reasons. One reason is to put people together for mentoring, encouraging, and instructions in righteousness. We should never underestimate the power of hands on training. I'm sure that some men who used their talent to work for the Lord went on to work with the same skill set for a living. Can you imagine having on your resume' that you put your craft to use for the building of the Tabernacle? Those who became masters of their work were recorded for their labor of love just as those of us who work in the house of the Lord today are recorded in the books in heaven for our labor of love.

Many Christians miss a great opportunity to grow and be blessed of the Lord by not working in the Church.

**First Sight of the Challenges before them to Inherit the Land.**

*Numbers 13:1 ¶ And the LORD spake unto Moses, saying,  2  Send thou men, that they may search the land of Canaan, which I give unto the children of Israel: of every tribe of their fathers shall ye send a man, every one a ruler among them. 3 And Moses by the commandment of the LORD sent them from the wilderness of Paran: all those men were heads of the children of Israel.*

Not many days from the Red Sea God had brought the Israelites from a company of slaves to a chosen people with a tabernacle, instructions on how to live and how to enter into His presence. Now he had them before the Promise Land to deliver it into their hands. He wanted the leaders to come back with a truthful report coupled with the faith that God would fulfill His promise to them right now!

*Numbers 13:26¶ And they went and came to Moses, and to Aaron, and to all the congregation of the children of Israel, unto the wilderness of Paran, to Kadesh; and brought back word unto them, and unto all the congregation, and shewed them the fruit of the land. 27 And they told him, and said, We came unto the land whither thou sentest us, and surely it floweth with milk and honey; and this is the fruit of it. 28 Nevertheless the people be strong that dwell in the land, and the cities are walled, and very great: and moreover we saw the children of Anak there. 29 The Amalekites dwell in the land of the south: and the Hittites, and the Jebusites, and the Amorites, dwell in the mountains: and the Canaanites dwell by the sea, and by the coast of Jordan. 30 And Caleb stilled the people before Moses, and said, Let us go up at once, and possess it; for we are well able to overcome it. 31 But the men that went up with him said, We be not able to go up against the people; for they are stronger than we. 32 And they brought up an evil report of the land which they had searched unto the children of Israel, saying, The land, through which we have gone to search it, is a land that eateth up the inhabitants thereof; and all the people that we saw in it are men of a great stature. 33 And there we saw the giants, the sons of Anak, which come of the giants: and we were in our own sight as grasshoppers, and so we were in their sight. 14:1 ¶ And all the congregation lifted up their voice, and cried; and the people wept that night. 2 And all the children of Israel murmured against Moses and against Aaron: and the whole congregation said unto them, Would God that we had died in the land of Egypt! or would God we had died in this wilderness!*

When Israel was at the threshold of entering into their promise, they were faced with many challenges that should not have gripped their hearts with fear. Rather, God wanted them to rely on Him further to obtain the land. Instead of looking at the evidence that proved God had brought them into a place flowing with milk and honey, they focused on how they saw themselves and their inabilities to accomplish such a lofty task. God wanted them to trust Him, rely on Him, and believe that he would never set anything before them that they could not accomplish with His leadership. God knew their capability with Him better than they did. This is why Proverbs 3:5 admonishes:

**Proverbs 3:5** *Trust in the LORD with all thine heart; and lean not unto thine own understanding.*

They believed the bad report and were not reasonable with Moses, Aaron, Joshua and Caleb's claim that the Lord would deliver the Canaanites into their hands. Fear had moved them into murmuring against Moses and they began to seek a leader that would lead them back to Egypt. God gave Joshua and Caleb the land because of their faith and cursed the rest of Israel to the wilderness until the old generation had died. Forty days of spying the land turned into forty more years in the wilderness. Who knows how many times and how long our destiny is delayed due to our failure to trust and obey the Lord in a timely manner? Let us keep our eyes on the capabilities of Jesus and not on our strength.

### Forty Years in the Wilderness

*Deuteronomy 8:2 And thou shalt remember all the way which the LORD thy God led thee these forty years in the wilderness, to humble thee, [and] to prove thee, to know what [was] in thine heart, whether thou wouldest keep His commandments, or no.*

God spoke to the younger generation that was to inherit the Promise Land on the purpose of the forty years. He knew that the forty years was a time to teach the next generation that they could trust God to deliver their enemies into their hands as long as they kept His commandments. God brought the next generation into battles to prove that he would fight their battles for them.

When they finally were able to go into Canaan's land, they would also send spies into the land. Did they learn from their forefathers' error?

*Joshua 2:1 ¶ And Joshua the son of Nun sent out of Shittim two men to spy secretly, saying, Go view the land, even Jericho. And they went, and came into an harlot's house, named Rahab, and lodged there.*
*Joshua 2:23 So the two men returned, and descended from the mountain, and passed over, and came to Joshua the son of Nun, and told him all [things] that befell them: 24 And they said unto Joshua, Truly the LORD hath delivered into our hands all the land; for even all the inhabitants of the country do faint because of us.*

The difference here is that the two spies brought a word of faith with knowledge that their enemies were faint of heart because of what they heard God was doing for the Israelites. When the enemy hears the things God has done, he has no hope to lean on, no one to whom he can run for help and no way to encourage himself against God's people. Their enemies' fear caused them to act in desperation and try to kill the spies to thwart the efforts of the Israelites.

God protected the spies with a harlot named Rahab. She afterwards became the wife of Salmon, a prince of the tribe of Judah and part of the genealogy of our Lord Jesus Christ.

## (III.) Canaan's Land

*Joshua 3: 15 And as they that bare the ark were come unto Jordan, and the feet of the priests that bare the ark were dipped in the brim of the water, (for Jordan overfloweth all his banks all the time of harvest,) 16 That the waters which came down from above stood and rose up upon an heap very far from the city Adam, that is beside Zaretan: and those that came down toward the sea of the plain, even the salt sea, failed, and were cut off: and the people passed over right against Jericho. 17 And the priests that bare the ark of the covenant of the LORD stood firm on dry ground in the midst of Jordan, and all the Israelites passed over on dry ground, until all the people were passed clean over Jordan.*

Once Israel had spent 40 years in the wilderness, God brought them over Jordan and into Canaan's Land. He brought them over Jordan by cutting off the water supply and parting the waters so that they would cross on dry ground, as did their fathers over the Red Sea. The parting of the Red Sea was a deliverance experience, while, the parting of Jordan was a developmental experience. The younger generation needed to develop the idea that they could move on God's command and that he would support them as he did their parents out of Egypt into the wilderness. Not only was this a testimony of God's commitment to Israel but also a sign for the inhabitants to fear the God of Israel even the more.

**SON**

God personified Israel, as a whole from Egypt to the Red Sea, as His son when he delivered them.

***Hosea 11:1*** ¶ *When Israel [was] a child, then I loved him, and called my son out of Egypt.*

Jesus said that he came not to destroy the law but to fulfill it. In order for Him to fulfill this prophecy, he had to be hidden from Herod in Egypt until he was called out of Egypt by His Father via angels.

***Matthew 2:15*** *And was there until the death of Herod: that it might be fulfilled which was spoken of the Lord by the prophet, saying, Out of Egypt have I called my son.*

**CHURCH**

God referred to Israel as a congregation when they were in the wilderness. This designation continued even into Canaan's Land. My focus here is on the transition from son to congregation or church. Thus implying a son's maturing had taken place.

***Exodus 12:1*** ¶ *And the LORD spake unto Moses and Aaron in the land of Egypt, saying,   2   This month [shall be] unto you the beginning of months: it [shall be] the first month of the year to you. 3   Speak ye unto all the **congregation** of Israel, saying, In the tenth [day] of this month they shall take to them every man a lamb, according to the house of [their] fathers, a lamb for an house:*

The Hebrew root word for congregation is עוּד "'uwd" (*ood) which* means testimony, testifier, or to bear witness. With all that Israel had seen God do on their behalf, they were truly witnesses of Him and His power.

Being a congregation is synonymous with being in the wilderness of testing and trials. It was the testing and trials that gave the congregation their witness. Jesus Himself spent forty days in the wilderness before His ministry began and at the end was tested.

Jesus' final third of His journey was to court His bride and prepare her for a new covenant. The final third of Israel's journey transitioned them from a congregation (Church) to Jesus' Bride as they moved into Canaan's Land.

## BRIDE

*Isaiah 62:4 Thou shalt no more be termed Forsaken; neither shall thy land any more be termed Desolate: but thou shalt be called **Hephzibah**, and thy land **Beulah**: for the LORD delighteth in thee, and thy land shall be married.*

Isaiah prophecies that Israel will be called Hephzibah and her land Beulah. Hephzibah in Hebrew is בָּה "yupx" "Chephtsiy" חֶפְצִיבָאּ (*kheftsee'baw*) which means "my delight is in her".

The Hebrew word for Beulah is בָּעַל "ba'al" (*baw-al'*) meaning marry, wife and to be married. Entering into Canaan's Land or Beulah Land is allegorical for entering into a marriage contract with the Bridegroom (Jesus Christ). This is a mature covenant. Any with a childish faith would never be allowed to enter until they matured. Is it any wonder that God is a jealous God over His bride? Israel became the natural bride to God when they entered into His promised land. When she began to serve other gods, she committed spiritual adultery.

Crossing over Jordan earmarked the transition into a land flowing with milk and honey. There were three major divisions of Israel's journey in Canaan's Land: **1. Possess the Land**, **2. Divide the Land**, and **3. Keep the Land**.

## 1    Possess the Land

*Exodus 23:29 I will not drive them out from before thee in one year; lest the land become desolate, and the beast of the field multiply against thee. 30 By little and little I will drive them out from before thee, until thou be increased, and inherit the land. 31 And I will set thy bounds from the Red sea even unto the sea of the Philistines, and from the desert unto the river: for I will deliver the inhabitants of the land into your hand; and thou shalt drive them out before thee. 32 Thou shalt make no covenant* *with them, nor with their gods. 33 **They** shall not dwell in thy land, lest they make thee sin against me: for if thou serve their gods, it will surely be a snare unto thee.*

God let them know that he wasn't going to give them the complete inheritance in one year because they weren't yet capable of dividing and keeping it. They needed to grow into their legacy so God portioned the land they would not lose after obtaining it. They did indeed own the land! However, this was a developmental work.

Possessing the land was no easy task, but through the power of God, they would succeed. Their experience in the wilderness taught them that nothing is too hard for God. This was a higher level of faith into which they had grown. The giants were no longer threatening; the walled cities were no longer invincible; the land was now conquerable and they weren't grasshoppers in their own sight. At their achieved level of maturity they went over Jordan and battled with a confidence mixed with the fear of God to be obedient.

***Joshua 1:10*** *¶ Then Joshua commanded the officers of the people, saying, **11** Pass through the host, and command the people, saying, Prepare you victuals; for within three days ye shall pass over this Jordan, to go in to possess the land, which the LORD your God giveth you to possess it. **12** And to the Reubenites, and to the Gadites, and to half the tribe of Manasseh, spake Joshua, saying, **13** Remember the word which Moses the servant of the LORD commanded you, saying, The LORD your God hath given you rest, and hath given you this land. **14** Your wives, your little ones, and your cattle, shall remain in the land which Moses gave you on this side Jordan; but ye shall pass before your brethren armed, all the mighty men of valour, and help them; **15** Until the LORD have given your brethren rest, as he hath given you, and they also have possessed the land which the LORD your God giveth them: then ye shall return unto the land of your possession, and enjoy it, which Moses the LORD's servant gave you on this side Jordan toward the sunrising.*

This was a place of maturity that God required of all in that they would selflessly take the land in unity even if some had already inherited their portion. It wasn't until all the land had been taken when the men could return to their portion God had given them. They were to be of one mind and in accord with God and each other because, working together was paramount at this stage. All needed to depend on the Lord and each other in order to succeed. As the land was taken, it was inherited or distributed to the other tribes of Israel after several years of possessing it from the enemy of God.

No one can reach this stage in his walk with God without learning to get in one accord with others in like faith with a common goal to serve the Lord. The church can only grow when saints band together in the spirit of unity. It's a sign of maturity to find unity in the house of God and lift up the vision of the pastor.

### Disobedience (to whom much is given, much is required)

*Luke 12:48 But he that knew not, and did commit things worthy of stripes, shall be beaten with few stripes. For unto whomsoever **much is given**, of him shall be much **required**: and to whom men have committed much, of him they will ask the more.*

In the natural course of things, Israel began to walk into the perfect will of God. This was due to Israel vowing to obey the Lord eternally and their maturity with Him. When one matures, the freedoms are increased along with the responsibilities. God made His response to disobedience known to the Israelites before they vowed to follow Him. When God pulled back from Israel after Achan trespassed against Him, all of Israel knew sin was in the camp; something was wrong.

*Joshua 7:1 ¶ But the children of Israel committed a trespass in the accursed thing: for Achan, the son of Carmi, the son of Zabdi, the son of Zerah, of the tribe of Judah, took of the accursed thing: and the anger of the LORD was kindled against the children of Israel.*

*Joshua 7:4 So there went up thither of the people about three thousand men: and they fled before the men of Ai. 5 And the men of Ai smote of them about thirty and six men: for they chased them [from] before the gate [even] unto Shebarim, and smote them in the going down: wherefore the hearts of the people melted, and became as water.*

*Joshua 7: 19* *And Joshua said unto Achan, My son, give, I pray thee, glory to the LORD God of Israel, and make confession unto him; and tell me now what thou hast done; hide [it] not from me. 20 And Achan answered Joshua, and said, Indeed I have sinned against the LORD God of Israel, and thus and thus have I done: 21 When I saw among the spoils a goodly Babylonish garment, and two hundred shekels of silver, and a wedge of gold of fifty shekels weight, then I coveted them, and took them; and, behold, they [are] hid in the earth in the midst of my tent, and the silver under it.*

*Joshua 7:25* *And Joshua said, Why hast thou troubled us? the LORD shall trouble thee this day. And all Israel stoned him with stones, and burned them with fire, after they had stoned them with stones. 26 And they raised over him a great heap of stones unto this day. So the LORD turned from the fierceness of his anger. Wherefore the name of that place was called, The valley of Achor, unto this day.*

*Joshua 8:1* ¶ *And the LORD said unto Joshua, Fear not, neither be thou dismayed: take all the people of war with thee, and arise, go up to Ai: see, I have given into thy hand the king of Ai, and his people, and his city, and his land:*

Israel, the bride of God, had allowed covetousness to replace obedience. Nothing being hidden from God, he could not wink at or ignore her sin. However, when Joshua sought out and removed the transgression from people of Israel, God restored the relationship to the point that they were able to take the land of Ai.

When we mature in Christ to the point where he is, we will begin destroying idols and religious folklore on a dynamic basis, knowing that coveting what God says is to be destroyed is a trap that must be avoided. However, when we fall into these temptations, we can repent and press on to a victorious walk.

### The Temptation of Binding Contracts without seeking God.

*Joshua 9:3* ¶ *And when the inhabitants of Gibeon heard what Joshua had* *done unto Jericho and to Ai,    4 They did work wilily, and went and made as if they had been ambassadors, and took old sacks upon their asses, and wine bottles, old, and rent, and bound up;    5 And old shoes and clouted upon their feet, and old garments upon them; and all the bread of their provision was dry [and] mouldy. 6 And they went to Joshua unto the camp at Gilgal, and said unto him, and to the men of Israel, We be come from a far country: now therefore make ye a league with us. 7 And the men of Israel said unto the Hivites, Peradventure ye dwell among us; and how shall we make a league with you?  8 And they said unto Joshua, We [are] thy servants. And Joshua said unto them, Who [are] ye? and from whence come ye?  9 And they said unto him, From a very far country thy servants are come because of the name of the LORD thy God: for we have heard the fame of him, and all that he did in Egypt,    10 And all that he did to the two kings of the Amorites, that [were] beyond Jordan, to Sihon king of Heshbon, and to Og king of Bashan, which [was] at Ashtaroth. 11 Wherefore our elders and all the inhabitants of our country spake to us, saying, Take victuals with you for the journey, and go to meet them, and say unto them, We [are] your servants: therefore now make ye a league with us. 12 This our bread we took hot [for] our provision out of our houses on the day we came forth to go unto you; but now, behold, it is dry, and it is mouldy:   13 And these bottles of wine, which we filled, [were] new; and, behold, they be rent: and these our garments and our shoes are become old by reason of the very long journey. 14 And **the men took of their victuals, and asked not [counsel] at the mouth of the LORD.** 15 ¶ And Joshua made peace with them, and made a league with them, to let them live: and the princes of the congregation sware unto them. 16 And it came to pass at the end of three days after they had made a league with them, that they heard that they [were] their neighbours, and [that] they dwelt among them. 17 And the children of Israel journeyed, and came unto their cities on the third day. Now their cities [were] Gibeon, and Chephirah, and Beeroth, and Kirjathjearim. 18 And the children of Israel smote them not, because the princes of the congregation had sworn unto them by the LORD God of Israel. And all the congregation murmured against the princes. 19 But all the princes said unto all the congregation, We have sworn unto them by the LORD God of Israel: now therefore we may not touch them.*

Appearances are very deceptive at this stage. When we walk in this place of possession, we must ensure that we are not embracing our enemy in a league that would hinder our walk and success. We need to remember to pray before entering into agreements with others. The primary root word in Hebrew for Hittites is חַתַת chathath (khaw-thath') which means to be dismayed, afraid, break in pieces, abolish, terrify and discouraged. Clearly the Lord wanted to destroy the Hittites out of their lives and ours!

2 Kings shows us that the very people they were in a league with grew and rose up to make war with Israel. How many times does the Lord require us to do something and we obey partially? The results can be devastating. This is a clear example of what can happen if we don't obey the Lord exactly how, when and where he directs us.

## 2  Divide the Land

As the land was taken, a portion was given to specific tribes. Dividing the land required that they take heed to God's instructions on division and then mark it accordingly. They were required to administer the land to their brothers as it was possessed.

While dividing the land, all the men of war were required to continue with the taking of the land while their families settled into their inheritance that had already been won.

*Numbers 33:54 And ye shall divide the land by lot for an inheritance among your families: [and] to the more ye shall give the more inheritance, and to the fewer ye shall give the less inheritance: every man's [inheritance] shall be in the place where his lot falleth; according to the tribes of your fathers ye shall inherit.*

*Deuteronomy 10:9 Wherefore Levi hath no part nor inheritance with his brethren; the LORD [is] his inheritance, according as the LORD thy God promised him.*

The only tribe that didn't inherit the land was the Levites because the Lord was their inheritance.

### 3    Keep the Land

After dividing the land, God required Israel to keep His statutes and the land they had received. He wanted to show the world what a nation under His leading could accomplish. Keeping an occupied land is very hard work because complacency will allow squatters (iniquities) to creep into the land.

The priests were required to offer continual sacrifices to atone for the sins of themselves and the people. Judgment was done continually to keep the relationship with God in good standing.

As you read about all the kings of the land, you will observe that they were directly responsible for keeping the things of God. Yet all of Israel was held accountable for the righteousness or iniquities brought into the land.

Let us be mindful that when we obtain a greater level in Him it is our responsibility to keep the land that we have achieved as well as go forward to take more land.

# 4

---

# THE PRIEST'S JOURNEY

## (FROM THE BRAZEN ALTAR TO THE MERCY SEAT)

Just as Israel traveled through three main stages to their final destination, the high priest also traveled through three stages to reach the closest position to God any man could achieve and remain living (See Figure 5). Egypt, the Wilderness, and Canaan's Land parallel the Courtyard, Holy Place and the Holy of Holies respectively in many ways. You should begin to see these preordained similarities along with the Christian's walk to spiritual growth more clearly as we cover these three stages.

We will be looking at each piece of furniture in the Mosaic Tabernacle and examinig the roles played and their meanings. We will also be looking at what Jesus did to become the more perfect tabernacle as stated in Hebrews chapter 9.

## (I.) THE COURTYARD (A PLACE OF JUDGEMENT).

The courtyard was the first of three major divisions of the tabernacle. The priests and all the congregation would enter through the gate into the courtyard. The people would praise the Lord in singing and prayer as they observed the priests performing their daily sacrifices on behalf of the themselves and the people. God required that there be a morning and evening sacrifice daily. Incidently, some sacrifices were not required daily but the Sin offering, Whole Burnt and Peace offerings were.

### Blood, Fire, and Water

Before the priests could enter into the Holy Place, a place that destroyed all who were unclean that entered, they needed their sins judged. Brass symbolizes judgement and God requres judgement before man can approach him in the Holy Place. A sacrifice was required to apply blood to atone for sin and fire was needed to fall from God to approve the sacrifice at the Brazen Altar. The water at the Laver was for the priests to wash the sacrifice, their hands, and their feet. Without the blood, fire and water experience, the priests would never survive entering into the Holy Place.

## THE BRAZEN ALTAR

*Exodus 27: 1 ¶ And thou shalt make an altar of shittim wood, five cubits long, and five cubits broad; the altar shall be foursquare: and the height thereof shall be three cubits. 2 And thou shalt make the horns of it upon the four corners thereof: his horns shall be of the same: and thou shalt overlay it with brass. 3 And thou shalt make his pans to receive his ashes, and his shovels, and his basons, and his fleshhooks, and his firepans: all the vessels thereof thou shalt make of brass. 4 And thou shalt make for it a grate of network of brass; and upon the net shalt thou make four brasen rings in the four corners thereof. 5 And thou shalt put it under the compass of the altar beneath, that the net may be even to the midst of the altar. 6 And thou shalt make staves for the altar, staves of shittim wood, and overlay them with brass. 7 And the staves shall be put into the rings, and the staves shall be upon the two sides of the altar, to bear it. 8 Hollow with boards shalt thou make it: as it was shewed thee in the mount, so shall they make it.*

*Ex 40:6 And thou shalt set the altar of the burnt offering before the door of the tabernacle of the tent of the congregation.*

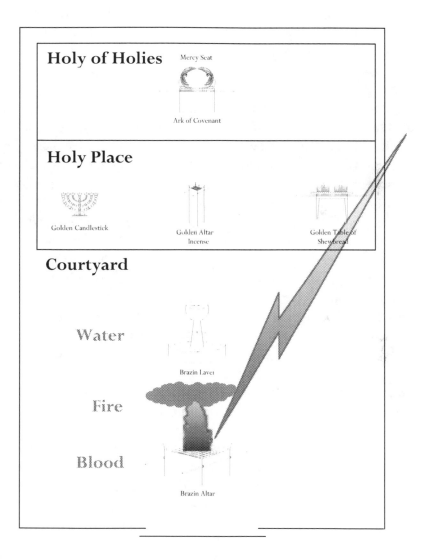

**Figure 5. Mosaic Tabernacle.**

Once through the gate of the tabernacle, the first piece of furniture approached was the Brazen Altar. This piece of furniture was made of shittim wood and overlaid with brass. This is where the blood and fire portion of the courtyard took place.

The Brazen Altar was four square. Even as one entered into the tabernacle, God wanted to give them a vision of the four square city, New Jerusalem. And as we enter into the courtyard by the blood of Jesus, he wants to give us a vision of entering into the New City. The Lord had no intention of having His people stop at the Brazin Altar. He meant for us to move into His presence at the Ark of the Covenant and Mercy Seat where His mercy resides.

*Proverbs 29:18 ¶ Where [there is] no vision, the people perish: but he that keepeth the law, happy [is] he.*

The Brazen Altar was also known as the Throne of Grace because the blood was poured here to atone for sins and affords grace to the one who approaches God. Grace is commonly known as unmerited favor. Mercy is commonly known as receiving better than we deserve. To be allowed the privilege to step into the presence of God is better than we deserve.

*Hebrews 4:16 Let us therefore come boldly unto the throne of grace, that we may obtain mercy, and find grace to help in time of need.*

The scripture above captures the complete process the High Priest took as he ascended from the Brazin Altar (Grace) to the Ark and Mercy Seat (Mercy) and then descended to the Brazin Altar (Grace). The frequency of our visits to the throne of grace should be as often as the priests sacrificed at the Brazin altar, morning and evening.

### Blood

Just as Israel applied blood to the lintel and side post to provide a blood cross to protect the inhabitants from the angel of death, the blood was poured out at the base and placed on the horns of the brazen altar twice a day to atone for the sins of all Israel. We receive our deliverance from the power of sin and death by receiving Jesus (the Blood) in our heart. His blood was shed once and for all on the cross for the salvation of those who will receive Christ. However, the blood was never meant to stop there, it was to be the catalyst to bring the believer to the Holy of Holies.

Among the many offerings that were offered at the brazen altar, I would like to focus on three of the most predominant offerings: the Sin, Whole Burnt, and Peace offering.

The portion of Jesus' blood that replaced the Sin offering is the blood that all Christians experience at salvation. The Whole burnt offering is experienced when a Christian chooses to wholly surrender every aspect of his life to God; this offering provokes God to answer by fire on the altar in the heart (Baptism of the Holy Ghost with the evidence of speaking in other tongues is the smoke). The Peace offering is an offering that the Christian must deliberately decided to rest in Christ's leading and is at peace with himself and his neighbor (a decision to forgive).

### Sin Offering

*Exodus 29:10 And thou shalt cause a bullock to be brought before the tabernacle of the congregation: and Aaron and his sons shall put their hands upon the head of the bullock. 11 And thou shalt kill the bullock before the LORD, by the door of the tabernacle of the congregation. 12 And thou shalt take of the blood of the bullock, and put it upon the horns of the altar with thy finger, and pour all the blood beside the bottom of the altar. 13 And thou shalt take all the fat that covereth the inwards, and the caul that is above the liver, and the two kidneys, and the fat that is upon them, and burn them upon the altar. 14 But the flesh of the bullock, and his skin, and his dung, shalt thou burn with fire without the camp: it is a sin offering.*

### Horns

The blood was put on the horns of the altar. The horns on an animal provide a defense and are used in aggression against any foes. They also were used as a display for mating season as a form of exaltation. Horns speak of aggression, defense and exaltation.

### Aggressive Blood

There is a portion of Christ's blood that is for aggressive spiritual warfare in your walk with Him. We find ourselves at times standing before the Lord saying "Lord, I know that I should do the right thing but my flesh wants to do the wrong thing. I need your aggressive blood to attack this thing in my heart so that I don't sin." This kind of transparency with the Lord and yourself causes the spiritual realm to resonate with victory for you.

### Defensive Blood

There are times when we need a defense on our behalf. Christ's blood placed on the horns on the altar in heaven provides a mighty defense for those who apply it to their situations. God will back up the blood of His son to the fullest extent.

### Exalted Blood

The blood on the horns also testifies that no sin is so high that the Blood of Christ can't cleanse. Jesus' blood was lifted on the cross to fulfill the sin offering.

The horns on the altar are for the portion of blood that we as Christians need to defend and be aggressive against the attacks of the enemy and iniquities in our heart.

### Blood of Low Degree

A portion of the blood was poured at the base of the altar where it would seep into the ground signifying that no sin was too low for the blood to cleanse. Jesus' blood was spilled on the ground to fulfill the sin offering. I believe that the point at which the sins of the world were transferred on Jesus was as he went to pray in the garden of Gethsemane. In Matthew 26:38, Jesus reveals that His soul is exceeding sorrowful, even unto death. The law of sin and death started to take hold on Jesus' body because he had taken on the sins of the world, past, present and

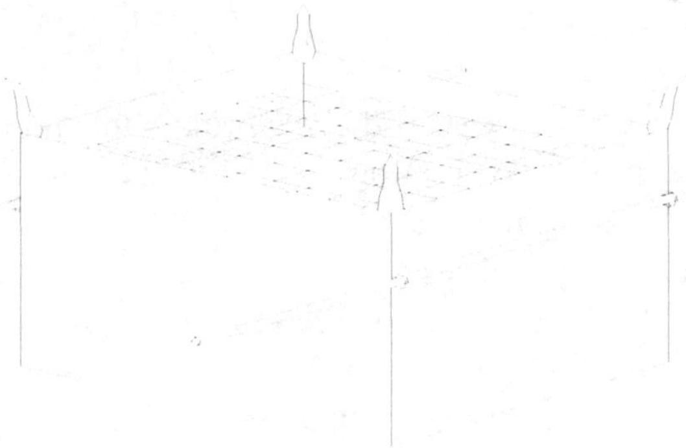

**Figure 6. Brazin Alter.**

future. Luke 22:43-44 reveals that after the angel from heaven strengthened Him that he prayed more earnestly and His sweat was as great drops of blood. Surely the weight of sin was taking a toll on His mortal body.

*Matthew 26: 36 ¶ Then cometh Jesus with them unto a place called Gethsemane, and saith unto the disciples, Sit ye here, while I go and pray yonder. 37 And he took with him Peter and the two sons of Zebedee, and began to be sorrowful and very heavy. 38 Then saith he unto them, My soul is exceeding sorrowful, even unto death: tarry ye here, and watch with me. 39 And he went a little further, and fell on his face, and prayed, saying, O my Father, if it be possible, let this cup pass from me: nevertheless not as I will, but as thou wilt.*

Jesus knew that the priests had to examine Him and lay hands on Him before he could fulfill the sin offering. If he had died at the garden then mankind would have been lost forever. With this reasoning, I am convinced that the cup that Jesus asked the Father to be passed from Him was the cup of death that stood before Him that very hour in the garden. Jesus taught the disciples on several occasions that he would be crucified and rise on the third day, yet he would not lift a finger to strengthen Himself to bring His word to pass as the law of sin and death weighed heavily on His body. What a show of humility!

Just as the remains of the sin offering were taken out of the camp, so were the remains of Jesus after he had been beaten and scourged was crucified outside the city. I pray that we will not be ashamed to suffer for Christ's sake inside and outside of the camp.

### Whole Burnt Offering

*Exodus 29: 16 And thou shalt slay the ram, and thou shalt take his blood, and sprinkle it round about upon the altar. 17 And thou shalt cut the ram in pieces, and wash the inwards of him, and his legs, and put them unto his pieces, and unto his head. 18 And thou shalt burn the whole ram upon the altar: it is a burnt offering unto the LORD: it is a sweet savour, an offering made by fire unto the LORD.*

The sacrifice was slain (blood), washed (water) and then the whole ram was offered to the Lord. This is the offering that would provoke God to answer by fire signifying His acceptance of the offering.

### Encircling Blood

Blood was sprinkled round about the altar to atone the complete perimeter along with the altar. Even the hedge that the Lord sets round about us is supported by His encircling blood.

Jesus fulfilled the Whole Burnt Offering because he was offered wholly upon the cross and would not exalt Himself or do anything that he did not receive from the Father. Jesus offered up His own will to the Father's will continually. He is the perfect whole burnt offering.

*John 5:19* *Then answered Jesus and said unto them, Verily, verily, I say unto you, The Son can do nothing of Himself, but what he seeth the Father do: for what things soever he doeth, these also doeth the Son likewise.*

This is the Christian's whole burnt offering to the Lord that they lay down their will for Jesus'. When a Christian surrenders his life completely to the Lord, it provokes God to answer by fire on the altar in their heart and the sweet smelling savor rises to the Lord. The baptism of the Holy Ghost with evidence of speaking in tongues is the fire upon the altar in a Christian's heart with the tongues being the smoke that rises unto the Lord as a sweet smelling savor.

*Ex 29:41* *And the other lamb thou shalt offer at even, and shalt do thereto according to the meat offering of the morning, and according to the drink offering thereof, for a sweet savour, an offering made by fire unto the LORD.*

### Peace Offering

Leviticus Chapter 3 covers the peace offering. This offering could be made with a bullock, cow, calf, sheep, goat, or lamb. The offering had to be without blemish. The peace offering was an offering made from a willing heart. Usually, it was offered simultaneously with sin and whole burnt offerings. The owner could be bringing a peace offering in gratitude of the mercy and grace received and/or in expectation of mercy and grace.

***Leviticus 4:35*** *And he shall take away all the fat thereof, as the fat of the lamb is taken away from the sacrifice of the peace offerings; and the priest shall burn them upon the altar, according to the offerings made by fire unto the LORD: and the priest shall make an atonement for his sin that he hath committed, and it shall be forgiven him.*

The fat, kidneys and caul was to be taken away and burnt on the altar separately; this was the Lord's portion. God claimed the fat for Himself. Fat responds to fire in a lively way. It pops, sizzles, and will move under the influence of the explosions of the bursting oil pockets. This is a representation of zeal. Zeal will cause a Christian to respond in praise and worship, seek the Lord carefully and diligently and finally clean up their house, inwardly and outwardly. This type of cleansing brings a covenant of peace. Zeal is a manifestation of our dedication and commitment. Before I continue with the subject of zeal, I want to give you a background of how serious the Lord is about his relationship with Israel.

***Deuteronomy 7: 2*** *And when the LORD thy God shall deliver them before thee; thou shalt smite them, and utterly destroy them; thou shalt make no covenant with them, nor shew mercy unto them: **3** Neither shalt thou make marriages with them; thy daughter thou shalt not give unto his son, nor his daughter shalt thou take unto thy son. **4 For they will turn away thy son from following me, that they may serve other gods:** so will the anger of the LORD be kindled against you, and destroy thee suddenly.*

Deuteronomy 7: 1-4 gives the commandment and the purpose for God not wanting Israel to marry the inhabitants of Canaan. Some have said that this is the commandment against mixed marriages. As long as the mix they are referring to delineates the saved with the unsaved, they are correct.

Moses married an Ethiopian woman, I am assuming she was dark skinned, and God was at peace with that because it never drew Moses away from Him. This is confirmed when Miriam and Aaron complained against it and God plagued Miriam (See Numbers 12). When I'm asked how to determine if a couple is unequally yoked, I start by asking them to examine if either will be drawn away from increasing their relationship with the Lord Jesus.

God is provoked to jealousy when His people give honor, praise, sacrifices and higher priority to other things in their lives. When His people move in zeal to correctly prioritize their lives according to the word of God, he responds with a covenant of peace.

Let's return to the subject of zeal.

**_Numbers 25: 6_** _¶ And, behold, one of the children of Israel came and brought unto his brethren a Midianitish woman in the sight of Moses, and in the sight of all the congregation of the children of Israel, who were weeping before the door of the tabernacle of the congregation._ **_7_** _And when Phinehas, the son of Eleazar, the son of Aaron the priest, saw it, he rose up from among the congregation, and took a javelin in his hand;_ **_8_** _And he went after the man of Israel into the tent, and thrust both of them through, the man of Israel, and the woman through her belly. So the plague was stayed from the children of Israel._ **_9_** _And those that died in the plague were twenty and four thousand._ **_10_** _And the LORD spake unto Moses, saying,_ **_11_** _Phinehas, the son of Eleazar, the son of Aaron the priest, hath turned my wrath away from the children of Israel, while_ **_he was zealous for my sake_** _among them, that I consumed not the children of Israel in my jealousy._ **_12_** _Wherefore say, Behold,_ **_I give unto him my covenant of peace_**_:_ **_13_** _And he shall have it, and his seed after him, even the covenant of an everlasting priesthood; because he was zealous for his God, and made an atonement for the children of Israel._

In order for the Midianite woman to be brought before the people who wept at the door of the tabernacle, she had to have been in the courtyard of the tabernacle. This was of great offense to the Lord. Phinehas' zeal saved Israel from complete destruction by the plague brought by Israel's spiritual adultery.

The word zeal in the Hebrew is קָנָא qana' (_kaw-naw'_) which translates to extreme jealousy, envy, and zeal. Also it means "to provoke to jealous anger".

Peace is a great thing to follow after. When we use our zeal to clean out the things that detract from our walk with Jesus, we are met by the Lord with peace, even from our enemies.

*Proverbs 16:7 ¶ When a man's ways please the LORD, he maketh even his enemies to be at peace with him.*

Proverbs 16:7 comes to mind when I find no peace with my enemies. I always reexamine myself first when I am under fire to ensure that it's really for Christ sake and not of my own sin.

The Lord looks for zeal in a saint that he can receive as an offering of fat from them. A quickening reminds me of zeal because it is an explosive reaction to a combination of elements that produce action.

*Romans 8:11 But if the Spirit of him that raised up Jesus from the dead dwell in you, he that raised up Christ from the dead shall* **also quicken your mortal bodies by his Spirit that dwelleth in you**.

When we offer up the fat of our peace offering to Jesus, we will find ourselves responding to Him in a lively manner because he causes us to be lively stones.

*1 Peter 2:5 Ye also, as* **lively stones**, *are built up a spiritual house, an holy priesthood, to offer up spiritual sacrifices, acceptable to God by Jesus Christ.*

When David danced before the Lord with all his might, I am convinced that he was offering up the fat of the peace offering in his dance. God responded to David's sacrifice of praise to the point that he was determined not to let his wife, whom he loved, mock him into retreating in his new found experience. David must have experienced a quickening from God.

The meat of the peace offering was burned on the altar and eaten by the priests and the owner. Those who ate of the peace offering were required to be clean according to the law. Isn't it interesting that the eating together with the priest and God consummated the peace offering? Let us eat at the Lord's Table and fellowship with Him in the peace that passes all understanding.

Jesus fulfilled this offering as our prince of peace.

**John 14:27** _Peace I leave with you, my peace I give unto you: not as the world giveth, give I unto you. Let not your heart be troubled, neither let it be afraid._

We must continually plead the blood on our lives that we might keep the peace that Jesus has afforded us. When we find ourselves troubled or afraid, we must seek a peace offering with the Lord. I pray that you will continue in the peace that Jesus gives.

**Fire:**

The Israelites witnessed the Lord's provision for supernatural fire several ways in the wilderness in the tabernacle. After Moses set up the tabernacle the Lord moved in to dwell with His people.

**Exodus 40: 34** ¶ _Then a cloud covered the tent of the congregation, and the glory of the LORD filled the tabernacle._ **35** _And Moses was not able to enter into the tent of the congregation, because the cloud abode thereon, and the glory of the LORD filled the tabernacle._ **36** _And when the cloud was taken up from over the tabernacle, the children of Israel went onward in all their journeys:_ **37** _But if the cloud were not taken up, then they journeyed not till the day that it was taken up._ **38** _For the cloud of the LORD was upon the tabernacle by day, and fire was on it by night, in the sight of all the house of Israel, throughout all their journeys._

This cloud funneled down from heaven, possibly similar to a tornado, until it rested on the Mercy Seat in the Holy of Holies and the glory of the Lord would fill the tabernacle. The priests and the people knew when to pack up for a move when they saw the cloud rise up off of the Mercy Seat and the glory would leave the tabernacle. As we sanctify our sanctuary (ourselves and our church building), we may see a visible cloud descend upon us.

There were two types of fire that existed at the Brazen Altar, the Continual Fire and The Fire from God.

## Continual Fire

After the first answer from God during the Whole burnt offering with fire in the mosaic tabernacle, the priests were required to maintain the fire in the Brazen Altar. This fire was started by God and every morning the priests were required to place wood in the altar, new incense on the Golden Altar of Incense, and new oil for the Golden Candlestick and more frankincense on the Golden Table of Shewbread.

***Leviticus6: 9*** *Command Aaron and his sons, saying, This is the law of the burnt offering: It is the burnt offering, because of the burning upon the altar all night unto the morning, and the fire of the altar shall be burning in it.*

***Leviticus 6: 12*** *And the fire upon the altar shall be burning in it; it shall not be put out: and the priest shall burn wood on it every morning, and lay the burnt offering in order upon it; and he shall burn thereon the fat of the peace offerings.* ***13*** *The fire shall ever be burning upon the altar;* ***it shall never go out.***

When we receive salvation, a fire is kindled in the Brazen Altar in our Hearts. Fire represents the Spirit of God. We must maintain this fire by making an offering in the evening and morning unto the Lord. This fire will lead us to a place in our walk that will bid us to make a whole burnt offering unto the Lord. If we will follow His leading we will experience an answer of consuming Fire from God.

To obey God's command to keep the fire burning, let us gather often with other fires of like precious faith. A hot coal alone will not stay hot for very long. However, if a coal is placed with other coals, even a cold coal will catch fire again.

## Fire from God

1 Corinthians 10:2 states that Israel was baptized in the cloud and the sea. The cloud referred to here is the Pillar of Cloud that overshadowed Israel by day and the Pillar of Fire that lit the sky for them by night. This was their Fire experience. The sea is the Red Sea which was their Water

experience which will be covered in more depth at the Brazin Laver.

In the Mosaic Tabernacle, supernatural fire would come from God to consume the whole burnt offering on the Brazen Altar on a daily basis. This was the way the priests knew that they could continue confidently into the Holy Place with their ministering to the Lord. This was the Fire experience.

*Leviticus 9:24 And there came a fire out from before the LORD, and consumed upon the altar the burnt offering and the fat: which when all the people saw, they shouted, and fell on their faces*

The sacrifice that provoked this kind of response from God was a whole burnt offering, the fire came from God when it was acceptable, and the smoke was a sweet smelling savor to the Lord.

1 Kings 18:21-40 tells of Elijah challenging the prophets of Baal and the prophets of the groves that ate at Jezebel's table. Elijah proclaimed that the God that answered by fire is the true God. As you read this account you'll see that Elijah rebuilt the old altar of the Lord and offered a whole burnt sacrifice at the same time of Israel's evening burnt sacrifice. You'll also find that he called the altar Israel which directed his offering for the atonement of Israel. He placed wood in the altar and dressed the bullock (**Blood**). Then he washed the whole burnt offering with twelve barrels of (**Water**), one for each tribe of Israel. He knew that God would simply do what he does every burnt sacrifice, answer by (**Fire**). I'm not trying to diminish the power that God gave to Elijah, rather conveying that his knowledge of God's principles enabled him to destroy the enemy in a huge way. Elijah was fully aware of the principle of the whole burnt offering, and with that, he destroyed many of Baal's prophets and believers.

Today, when we offer ourselves wholly unto the Lord, he will answer by fire on the altar of our hearts. The evidence of speaking in an unknown tongue is the smoke that rises up to God as a sweet smelling savor. This fire aids us in confidently moving towards the Holy Place so that we can minister to the Lord.

## THE BRAZEN LAVER

*Exodus 38:8 And he made the laver [of] brass, and the foot of it [of] brass, of the looking glasses of [the women] assembling, which assembled [at] the door of the tabernacle of the congregation.*

*Ex 40:7 And thou shalt set the laver between the tent of the congregation and the altar, and shalt put water therein.*

The Brazen Laver was constructed of shittah wood and then overlaid with highly polished brass. This brass was originally the mirrors that the women would use. Nowhere else was the looking glass of the women used in the Mosaic Tabernacle. This caused the priests to see themselves as they washed continually at the Laver. It is apparent here that God wanted the priests to judge themselves before they went into the Holy Place. Judgment is vital to the successful ascension into the Holy Place. Similarly, if we look into our own hearts as we live on this earth and ask for forgiveness, we will find no judgment in Heaven.

The actual size of the Brazen Laver was never revealed in the word of God. Water represents the word of God. I believe that God had no intentions of limiting the height, depth and breadth of His word, thus the size was not revealed. Also, the Brazen Laver had water in the basin above and in the foot below. The Brazen Laver resembles the height and depth of the word in its ability to carry out its portion of purging and cleaning that he was assigned. Some things in our lives can only be purged and cleansed by the power provided by the water experience.

### Water

The third portion of Israel's deliverance from Egypt came in the way of the Red Sea. According to 1 Corinthians 10:1-4, the Israelites were baptized unto Moses through the sea before they entered into the second third of their journey. Also, the enemy was destroyed when they tried to pursue the Israelites. Truly the water provides further separation from the world. This was their water experience.

The Brazen Laver provided the water experience for the priests as they prepared to enter into the second third (middle section) of the Mosaic

**Figure 7. Brazen Laver**

Tabernacle, the Holy Place. Here the light of the Golden Candlestick is the only source of light. The element of water separated the priests from the outside light and brought them into the light of the golden candlestick.

We can rest assured that when we get baptized and continue to wash our minds in the word, we will begin to walk by the light of the candlestick and not the light of the world. (See paragraph Golden Candlestick)

*Numbers 8:5 ¶ And the LORD spake unto Moses, saying, 6 Take the Levites from among the children of Israel, and cleanse them. 7 And thus shalt thou do unto them, to cleanse them: Sprinkle water of purifying upon them, and let them shave all their flesh, and let them wash their clothes, and [so] make themselves clean.*

*Exodus 30: 21 So they shall wash their hands and their feet, that they die not: and it shall be a statute for ever to them, even to him and to his seed throughout their generations.*

The priests were completely washed to cleanse them for the consecration as priests and then they washed daily their hands and their feet before entering into the Holy Place. The washing speaks of baptism in water and the washing of their hands and feet speaks of cleansing by the word of God daily. Hands represent our deeds and feet represent our walk before the Lord. Entering into the Holy Place without the Blood, Fire and Water is a deadly mistake.

The brass used on the Laver was from the looking glass of the women, so the priests would look into a mirror while they washed and would see what manner of men they were before entering into the Holy Place. The mirror of the word always reflects our personal dispositions, attitudes and sins before us. This is a time of inward comparison of our heart to the word of God. Inward judgement must be done before entering into our Holy Place.

*James 1: 21   Wherefore lay apart all filthiness and superfluity of naughtiness, and receive with meekness the engrafted word, which is able to save your souls. 22  But be ye doers of the word, and not hearers only, deceiving your own selves. 23  **For if any be a hearer of the word, and*** *not a doer, he is like unto a man beholding his natural face in a glass:* **24 For he beholdeth himself, and goeth his way, and straightway forgetteth what manner of man he was. 25** *But whoso looketh into the perfect law of liberty, and continueth therein, he being not a forgetful hearer, but a doer of the work, this man shall be blessed in his deed.*

Let us persue baptism and continual washing by the word of God so that we can enter into the next step of spiritual maturity, the Holy Place.

Baptism is essential for us as Christians. We need to be buried with Christ. The water has a purging power of its own and we will need it as we journey into our Wilderness / Holy Place experience.

*Isaiah 28:9* ¶ *Whom shall he teach knowledge? and whom shall he make to understand doctrine? them that are weaned from the milk, and drawn from the breasts. 10 For precept must be upon precept, precept upon precept; line upon line, line upon line; here a little, and there a little: 11 For with stammering lips and another tongue will he speak to this people.*

To make it in the Holy Place is to be weaned from the milk and drawn from the breasts. When we have obtained a working knowledge of the principles of the doctrine of Christ as stated in Hebrews 6:1-2, and have the Blood, Fire and Water experience, we qualify to move into the Holy Place where wisdom, understanding and knowledge is obtained. The Holy Place is no place for spiritual babes.

## (II.) THE HOLY PLACE

After the sacrifices were complete (Blood) and the Lord's acceptance was signified by supernatural fire consuming the sacrifice upon the altar (Fire), the priests would have already been, or then continued, to the Brazin Laver to wash his feet and hands (Water). With the judgement of sins complete, it was time for the priest to go into the Holy Place through the door of the tent, the people would remain in the courtyard. This is indicative that we understand God will always call us out to further separate us to Himself as we mature in Christ.

The cross is constructed of two bars, one vertical and the other horizontal. The verticle bar represents exaltation and the horizontal bar represents humility. The human body is parrallel with this horizontal bar when it is prostrate or laying down. And so the second third of the Mosaic Tabernacle, the Holy Place, was a place of humility. Here I'd like to point out that in the wilderness experience (the second third of Israel's journey) God provided the horizontal prayer bar or humility to provide a way of escape during trials and temptations. Whenever we find ourselves in a test or trail, if we will humble ourselves, fall on our face prostrate and seek Jesus' face, he will provide the strength and way of escape that we so desperately need.

Spending time in the Holy Place positions one at the heart of the cross and at the heart of God.

### Strange Fire

*Leviticus 9:23 ¶ And Moses and Aaron went into the tabernacle of the congregation, and came out, and blessed the people: and the glory of the LORD appeared unto all the people. 24 And there came a fire out from before the LORD, and consumed upon the altar the burnt offering and the fat: which when all the people saw, they shouted, and fell on their faces. 10:1 ¶ And Nadab and Abihu, the sons of Aaron, took either of them his censer, and put fire therein, and put incense thereon, and offered strange fire before the LORD, which he commanded them not. 2 And there went out fire from the LORD, and devoured them, and they died before the LORD. 3 ¶ Then Moses said unto Aaron, This is it that the LORD spake, saying, I will be sanctified in them that come nigh me, and before all the people I will be glorified. And Aaron held his peace.*

It must have been awsome to see God answered by fire for the first time before all the congregation. However, when God does the miraculus, it's no time to do something not commanded by Him. Praise and Worship would have been more appropriate for Nadab and Abihu. They both knew that the censors and Golden Altar of Incense were for burning Incense and that the Golden Candlestick needed to be lit but God had not given them the commandment to do so at this point.

It is of my belief that this fire from God was the only fire permitted in the tabernacle. Once the fire in the Brazin Altar was lit, it was to be maintained by the Levites. Once lit by the fire from the Brazin Altar, the

Golden Altar of Incense would be maintained by daily portions of new Incense. After the Golden Candlestick was lit with God's fire, he would be maintained by new oil. The frankencense on the Golden Table of Shewbread was lit with the same fire and then maintained with new portions of the same.

Hence this subject underlines the importance of having the Baptism of the Holy Ghost with evidence of speaking in other tongues. There are many types of fire which can be confused with the fire of God, let us give the whole burnt sacrifice to receive the true fire of God before we try to enter into the Holy Place in the tabernacle in our own heart. Anything else could result in spiritual suicide.

## THE GOLDEN ALTAR OF INCENSE

*Exodus 30:1 ¶ And thou shalt make an altar to burn incense upon: of shittim wood shalt thou make it. 2 A cubit shall be the length thereof, and a cubit the breadth thereof; foursquare shall it be: and two cubits shall be the height thereof: the horns thereof shall be of the same. 3 And thou shalt overlay it with pure gold, the top thereof, and the sides thereof round about, and the horns thereof; and thou shalt make unto it a crown of gold round about. 4 And two golden rings shalt thou make to it under the crown of it, by the two corners thereof, upon the two sides of it shalt thou make it; and they shall be for places for the staves to bear it withal. 5 And thou shalt make the staves of shittim wood, and overlay them with gold. 6 And thou shalt put it before the vail that is by the ark of the testimony, before the mercy seat that is over the testimony, where I will meet with thee. 7 And Aaron shall burn thereon sweet incense every morning: when he dresseth the lamps, he shall burn incense upon it.*

*Ex 40:5 And thou shalt set the altar of gold for the incense before the ark of the testimony, and put the hanging of the door to the tabernacle.*

The first piece of furniture that would be approached in the Holy Place is the Golden Altar of Incence. Here the priest would take care of the order of incense and offer prayers unto the Lord for themselves and all Israel.

The Golden Altar of Incense was constructed of shitta wood and overlaid with pure gold. Incense was prepared and burned continually and represented the prayers of the siants.

Incidently, here is were Zacharias was told that Elisabeth, his wife, was pregnant. Keep in mind that anything in the Holy Place that remains alive is Holy before the Lord. So when he doubted, Gabriel made him def and mute because of his unbelief (Luke 1:5-22).

As you can see, the Golden Altar of Incense, or prayer, is at the heart of the tabernacle. In fact, if one were to lay Jesus over the tabernacle, they would find that His heart would rest over the Golden Altar of Incense. I believe that God intended for prayer to be at the heart of His ministry. If we want to touch Jesus' heart, we must pray. Prayer is as holy incense smoldering, allowing the smoke to raise into the nostriles of God as a sweet smelling savour. There are times when I pray that I have smelled an unusual smell of what I perceive to be the incense of the Lord as he interceeds for us to the Father at Golden Altar of Incense in Heaven. What an inspiring experience!

The fire that was brought to the Golden Altar of Incense came from the fire that God sent to answer the whole burnt offering at the Brazin Altar. This fire was holy unto the Lord because it was sent from a portion of Himself to man.

There are three main forms of prayer that took place at this piece of furniture: Asking in knowledge, Intercession, and Travailing. Later I will discuss the difference and importance of each. Lets earmark this intersection at the Altar of Incense as a hub for the work of any ministry.

## THE GOLDEN CANDLE STICK

*Exodus 25:31 ¶ And thou shalt make a candlestick of pure gold: of beaten work shall the candlestick be made: his shaft, and his branches, his bowls, his knops, and his flowers, shall be of the same. 32 And six branches shall come out of the sides of it; three branches of the candlestick out of the one side, and three branches of the candlestick out of the other side: 33 Three bowls made like unto almonds, with a knop and a flower in one branch; and three bowls made like almonds in the other branch, with a knop and a flower: so in the six branches that come out of the candlestick. 34 And in the candlestick shall be four bowls made like unto almonds, with their knops and their flowers. 35 And there shall*

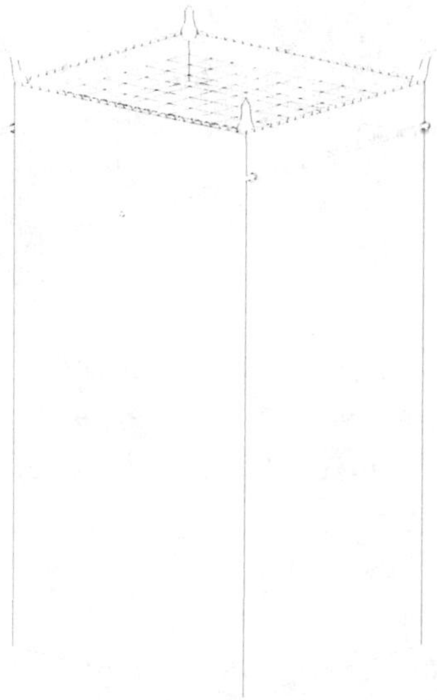

**Figure 8. Golden Altar of Incense.**

*be a knop under two branches of the same, and a knop under two branches of the same, and a knop under two branches of the same, according to the six branches that proceed out of the candlestick. 36 Their knops and their branches shall be of the same: all it shall be one beaten work of pure gold. 37 And thou shalt make the seven lamps thereof: and they shall light the lamps thereof, that they may give light over against it. 38 And the tongs thereof, and the snuffdishes thereof, shall be of pure gold. 39 Of a talent of pure gold shall he make it, with all these vessels. 40 And look that thou make them after their pattern, which was shewed thee in the mount.*

*Exodus 40:24 And he put the candlestick in the tent of the congregation, over against the table, on the side of the tabernacle southward. 25 And he lighted the lamps before the LORD; as the LORD commanded Moses.*

### A Beaten Work

*Hebrews 5:8 Though he were a Son, yet learned he obedience by the things which he suffered; 9 And being made perfect, he became the author of eternal salvation unto all them that obey Him;*

The Golden Candlestick was the one of two pieces that were beaten into the form God had specified. Jesus fullfiled this portion because he was a beaten work. Isaiah prophesied of his bruises and chastisement because God knew that Jesus had to fulfill the beaten work.

*Isaiah 53:5 But he [was] wounded for our transgressions, [he was] bruised for our iniquities: the chastisement of our peace [was] upon him; and with his stripes we are healed.*

As we mature in our walk with Christ, we will find that we will take part in a portion of what Jesus experienced in His sufferings. Although we may not readily admit that we are blessed to have taken part in what the Lord has suffered, we will see the truth as we begin to see the fruit of the suffering we endoured. Our calling requires that we be prepared and willing to suffer for Chirst's sake.

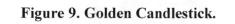

**Figure 9. Golden Candlestick.**

*1 Peter 4:1 ¶ Forasmuch then as Christ hath suffered for us in the flesh, arm yourselves likewise with the same mind: for he that hath suffered in the flesh hath ceased from sin;*

Jesus submitted Himself to the things he suffered because he beheld greater things to come. His obedience should inspire us to obey Him. Truly He was the son of God! Only the Messiah can fulfil all these details to such an exact measure!

### The Candlestick was a picture of the Word of God.

If one were to reconstruct the candlestick according to Exodus 25: 31-40, it would look like the one shown in Figure 9.

The number of lights is seven which is the number of completion. God rested the sabbath (seventh) day after he had completed creating the heavens and the earth. The candlestick represented complete light in the Holy Place and the fire that was brought to the candlestick came from the fire that God sent to answer the whole burnt offering at the Brazin Altar. This light was not the same light that was available in the courtyard. Light can be used allegorically to depict a point of view. In the Courtyard, natural sun light was available with the shadow of the pillar of cloud by day and a better light by night from the pillar of Fire. As the priests entered into the Holy Place, they were given complete light from the candlestick to walk by. This is the place were one can see things from the heart of God. When Jesus shines His light of the word on our lives, all things become clear and unobstucted. The psalmist had a revelation of the true meaning of the candlestick when he wrote:

*Psalms 119:105 NUN. Thy word is a lamp unto my feet, and a light unto my path.*

If one were to count the number of Almonds, Knobs and Flowers, they would arive at a total of 66. Thus Moses prophesied that God's complete light or word would exist as sixty six books in the Bible. This helps us identify what "all scripture" is encompassed in 2$^{nd}$ Timothy 3:16-17. Today, the lamp unto our feet and light unto our path still remains to be the word of God. We must seek to glean the portion of God's word to enlighten our feet so that we know our current position and the steps to see clearly so that we can walk accordingly.

*2 **Timothy** 3:16   All scripture is given by inspiration of God, and is profitable for doctrine, for reproof, for correction, for instruction in righteousness:   17   That the man of God may be perfect, throughly furnished unto all good works.*

Many works are inspired of the Lord. But if we only had the Bible, it would be sufficient to help us reach the measure and the stature of Jesus Christ as stated in Ephesians 4:13. The sixty six books of the bible throughly furnishes us all that we need. "Throughly Furnished" in verse 17 is an early nineteenth century phrase that connotes being struck in the center or core as an arrow hits the center of its target. We are furnished to the very core of our will first and then outwardly. How much more should we be taking the Word of God inwardly to impose an outward transformation?

Jesus fulfiled the candlestick because he is the word of God made flesh. As stated in John 1:1 & 14, Jesus is the Word of God.

*John 1:1 ¶ In the beginning was the Word, and the Word was with God, and the Word was God. 2 The same was in the beginning with God.*

*John 1:14 And the Word was made flesh, and dwelt among us, (and we beheld His glory, the glory as of the only begotten of the Father,) full of grace and truth.*

### The Priest's Duties.

*Leviticus 24:1 ¶ And the LORD spake unto Moses, saying, 2 Command the children of Israel, that they bring unto thee pure oil olive beaten for the light, to cause the lamps to burn continually. 3 Without the vail of the testimony, in the tabernacle of the congregation, shall Aaron order it from the evening unto the morning before the LORD continually: it shall be a statute for ever in your generations. 4 He shall order the lamps upon the pure candlestick before the LORD continually.*

The priests would move from the Golden Altar of Incense to the Golden Candlestick. They would trim the wicks and keep the lamps filled with oil and burning continually. The candlestick never went out just as the light of the word of God never extinguishes. I pray that we all are diligent in seeking the light of His wonderful word.

**GOLDEN TABLE OF SHEWBREAD**

*Exodus 25:23* ¶ *Thou shalt also make a table [of] shittim wood: two cubits [shall be] the length thereof, and a cubit the breadth thereof, and a cubit and a half the height thereof. 24 And thou shalt overlay it with pure gold, and make thereto a crown of gold round about. 25 And thou shalt make unto it a border of an hand breadth round about, and thou shalt make a golden crown to the border thereof round about. 26 And thou shalt make for it four rings of gold, and put the rings in the four corners that are on the four feet thereof. 27 Over against the border shall the rings be for places of the staves to bear the table. 28 And thou shalt make the staves of shittim wood, and overlay them with gold, that the table may be borne with them. 29 And thou shalt make the dishes thereof, and spoons thereof, and covers thereof, and bowls thereof, to cover withal: of pure gold shalt thou make them. 30 And thou shalt set upon the table shewbread before me alway.*

*Ex 40:24 And he put the candlestick in the tent of the congregation, over against the table, on the side of the tabernacle southward.*

The Golden Table of Shewbread was made of shittim wood and overlaid with gold. It was used to place the meal offering or unleavened bread for the priests to strengthen themselves as they ministered to the Lord in the Holy Place. The crown was to keep the bread and utensils from falling to the ground. Staves were used to carry the table when the cloud and fire lead them to their next destination in the journey.

*Numbers 4:7 And upon the table of shewbread they shall spread a cloth of blue, and put thereon the dishes, and the spoons, and the bowls, and covers to cover withal: and the continual bread shall be thereon:*

**Figure 10. Golden Table of Shewbread.**

*Leviticus 24:5  And thou shalt take fine flour, and bake twelve cakes thereof: two tenth deals shall be in one cake. 6 And thou shalt set them in two rows, six on a row, upon the pure table before the LORD. 7 And thou shalt put pure frankincense upon each row, that it may be on the bread for a memorial, even an offering made by fire unto the LORD. 8 Every sabbath he shall set it in order before the LORD continually, being taken from the children of Israel by an everlasting covenant. 9 And it shall be Aaron's and his sons'; and they shall eat it in the holy place: for it is most holy unto him of the offerings of the LORD made by fire by a perpetual statute.*

Two stacks of six loaves were placed on the table. God governed Israel by dividing them into twelve tribes. Twelve is the number of government and the purpose of the Table of Shewbread was to aid in the Priests ability to govern themselves according to the priestly statutes. The Priests would faint under the labor of their work if they didn't take of the bread of faith.

Faith is dependent on our ability to bring back to our memory the word of God and what he has done for us in the past. The frankincense was placed as a memorial which was to bring back to the priest's remembrance the strength of the Lord. This portion of the word is able to bring faith and strength for the performance of His word.

Just as the people provided the loaves for the priests, so should the church members provide for their man of God. So many times ministers of the gospel faint for lack of strength due to partitioners failing to supply their pastors with the bread they need to be strenghtened for a continual work. This bread not only refers to food, but money, tasks, help, administrations and any other kind act that would come from the heart. The minister is responsible for pouring his life out for the people to live and the people are responsible for assisting in pouring back into him so that he has enough to pour out again the next service. Did you notice that new bread was brought weekly? The remaining bread was set aside for the Levites and their family when it was replaced by the new cakes of bread on the sabbath. If your wondering how often the people gave to their priests, we can safely say that the minimum was once a week.

Fankincense was burned above the loaves in the Holy Place. The fire that was brought to the Golden Table of Shewbread came from the fire that God sent to answer the whole burnt offering at the Brazin Altar. This holy fire burned the frankincense that smoldered over the loaves and permeated the bread. Frankensense represents faith, I believe that this incense permeated the bread flavoring it with Faith. As the Priests ate of this bread, it is the faith that strengthened them to continue their arduouse work in the Holy Place.

### Unleavened Bread was the Meat Offering from the people.

The unleavened bread was bread without yeast. Leaven or yeast was considered unholy. Any bread with yeast was unfit for the tabernacle. It was received from the people as a meat offering and then placed on the table. The frankincense was placed on top of the two rows of bread and the smoke would permeate the bread.

_**John 6:35**  And Jesus said unto them, I am the bread of life: he that cometh to me shall never hunger; and he that believeth on me shall never thirst._

Jesus is our unleavened bread in the heavenly tabernacle. He fulfilled the service of the Golden Table of Shewbread by offering Himself as the bread of life. It is my belief that frankincense is symbolic of faith. Jesus is the full stature of faith, he is our frankincence. As we allow His word to permiate our lives it will strengthen our faith and allow us to walk in His light and continue in His work.

### Salt

_**Leviticus 2:11** ¶ No meat offering, which ye shall bring unto the LORD, shall be made with leaven: for ye shall burn no leaven, nor any honey, in any offering of the LORD made by fire. **12**  As for the oblation of the firstfruits, ye shall offer them unto the LORD: but they shall not be burnt on the altar for a sweet savour. **13**  And every oblation of thy meat offering shalt thou season with salt; neither shalt thou suffer the salt of the covenant of thy God to be lacking from thy meat offering: with all thine offerings thou shalt offer salt. **14**  And if thou offer a meat offering of thy firstfruits unto the LORD, thou shalt offer for the meat offering of_ *thy firstfruits green ears of corn dried by the fire, even corn beaten out of full ears. 15 And thou shalt put oil upon it, and lay frankincense thereon: it is a meat offering. 16 And the priest shall burn the memorial of it, part of the beaten corn thereof, and part of the oil thereof, with all the frankincense thereof: it is an offering made by fire unto the LORD.*

Interestingly enough that salt was required for the meat offering. Being a doer of the word seasons us with salt. Salt has cleansing and preserving properties that the Lord is very interested in. He wants to cleanse and preserve us. When we practice the word of God in every area of our lives, we are seasoned with salt from the Holy Ghost. This is how we become the salt of the earth.

*Matthew 5:13 ¶ Ye are the salt of the earth: but if the salt have lost his savour, wherewith shall it be salted? it is thenceforth good for nothing, but to be cast out, and to be trodden under foot of men.*

History has it that to enter into a salt covenant with someone is to partake of his hospitality, to derive subsistence from him; and hence the host who did so was bound to look after his guest's best interests. We must enter a salt covenant with the Lord to partake of His hospitality, to derive subsistence from him and to be bound to look after the Lord's interests and he ours.

### David ate the Shewbread.

David, the son of Jesse of the tribe of Judah, would not ordinarily be privileged to eat of this bread because he was not of the tribe of Levi. But God in His great mercy, allowed David and his men to eat and be strengthened that they would survive as they fled from the evil hand of Saul. Although they were given a privilege, they were still required to abstain from intimacy with their wives before they could eat of the holy bread.

*1 Samuel 21:2 And David said unto Ahimelech the priest, The king hath commanded me a business, and hath said unto me, Let no man know any thing of the business whereabout I send thee, and what I have commanded thee: and I have appointed [my] servants to such and such a place. 3 Now therefore what is under thine hand? give [me] five [loaves of] bread in mine hand, or what there is present. 4 And the priest answered David, and said, [There is] no common bread under mine hand, but there is hallowed bread; if the young men have kept themselves at least from women. 5 And David answered the priest, and said unto him, Of a truth women [have been] kept from us about these three days, since I came out, and the vessels of the young men are holy, and [the bread is] in a manner common, yea, though it were sanctified this day in the vessel. 6 So the priest gave him hallowed [bread]: for there was no bread there but the shewbread, that was taken from before the LORD, to put hot bread in the day when it was taken away.*

It was the mercy of God that enabled David to eat the shewbread that was set aside for the priests. Jesus continually gives us things that are intended for priests in order to sustain us on our journey to our predestination. What a merciful God we serve!

**The Priests Duties.**

In order to do that which pertained to the Golden Table of Shewbread, the priest would stop by the Golden Altar of Incense from the Golden Candlestick and offer prayer before proceeding to the Golden Table of Shewbread. The time spent in the Holy Place was considerable and the priests would eat of this frankinsense saturated bread to strengthen them that they would be able to govern themselves according to the law and complete the work.

*Proverbs 16:32 ¶ [He that is] slow to anger [is] better than the mighty; and he that ruleth his spirit than he that taketh a city.*

Governing oneself requires the strength that comes only from this portion of word of God. Once received and eaten, we are then able to rule our spirit and complete our work.

# (III.) HOLY OF HOLIES

The High Priest entered into the Holy of Holies once a year on the Day of Atonement. He would work from the Brazen Altar to the Ark of Covenant and the Mercy Seat. Once the ministry in the Holy Place was complete, the High Priest would find himself at the Golden Altar of Incense praying one last time before he would go past the veil into the Holy of Holies. Approaching the awesome presence of the Lord was a serious matter. God had the cherubim set in order upon the Mercy Seat to destroy anything unholy that approached Him. The High Priest would live or die by his obedience to God's statutes in the Holy of Holies, nothing more and nothing less. We can perceive that praying one last time before entering in was a deliberate and necessary act before crawling under the veil. He would have a sensor full of incense from the Golden Altar of Incense and Blood from the sacrifice. He was required to wave the incense before the Ark of Covenant and Mercy Seat and sprinkle the blood on the Ark and Mercy Seat. What a fearful and exhilarating experience it must have been, to be standing at the threshold of seeing a portion of God that only the High Priest could experience.

***Exodus 33:20*** *And he said, Thou canst not see my face: for there shall no man see me, and live.*

Only one High Priest per generation would approach this close to the glory of God. The blood was to consecrate the priest and protect him from sure destruction when he approached the Lord. The incense was to cloud the glory as a filter so that the priest would not be overwhelmed of the pureness of God's glory as well as bring the prayers of the people before His majestic presence in the Holy of Holies.

Once finished in the Holy of Holies, the high priest would return the same way he approached the Ark and Mercy Seat until he was back among the mortal. What a sobering experience it must have been to have climbed to the immortal one and then to return to mortal associations with its many cares. His perspective must have been more like God's.

As leaders in the church, we must remember that we will leave the church the same way we came in, we must always enter the church already edified. Not to say that the Lord doesn't meet the needs of His leaders, only that the spirit of the leader has a huge influence on the height of the service.

The light provided in the Holy of Holies is a profound light. Earlier, light was referred to as a point of view. In the courtyard, natural light was in abundance to represent the world's point of view, it's abundance of opinions and philosophies. The Holy Place was illuminated with the candlestick and the light here represented the heart of God, prayer illuminates us to what touches the heart of God. In the Holy of Holies, no natural light was produced here. The only light available was from the spiritual realm. This is the place to find the mind of God.

*Philippians 2:5 Let this mind be in you, which was also in Christ Jesus:*

Jesus walks in the Holy of Holies in the tabernacle in heaven. When He was in His ministry here on earth, He continued to stay in line with the Father's mind as He walked. Jesus said that he could only do what He saw the Father do. Not only did He know the mind of the Father, He also saw the Father perform His will.

### God Has His Own Pavilions of Darkness for His Purpose

In the Holy of Holies the only light available is the glory of God. Conceivably, natural darkness resides around the Ark and Mercy Seat. When we think of darkness, we may associate it with night time, a time to sleep, mystery, obscurity, the darkness of one's heart, evil, and even danger. These meanings exist in the word of God. However, if I can take a moment to modify what we normally recognize as darkness, I'd like to point out that the scriptures show that God has a darkness that doesn't fall under any of these definitions for the believer. Let's look at Psalms 18:11;

*Psalms 18:11 He made **darkness** ( חשך choshek ) his **secret place** ( סתר cether); his pavilion round about Him [were] dark waters [and] thick clouds of the skies.*

*2Sa 22:12 And he made **darkness** ( חשך choshek ) pavilions round about him, dark waters, and thick clouds of the skies.*

The Hebrew word for this kind of **Darkness** חשך choshek *(kho-shek')* is defined as darkness, dark, obscurity, night, **secret place**.

If God is surrounded by pavilions of darkness and makes them His secret place, then as we approach Him it seems logical that at some time during our approach, we will go through His pavilions of darkness. I want to emphasize **His** pavilions of darkness because as we look closer on this subject we will find that God has several wonderful purposes for **His** pavilions of darkness.

However, first we must realize that Psalms 18:11 defines God's secret place as darkness. The same Hebrew word for secret place in Psalms 18:11 is also found in Ps 91:1.

*Ps 91:1 ¶ He that dwelleth in the **secret place** ( סתר cether) of the most High shall abide under the shadow of the Almighty.*

This **Secret Place** is the Hebrew word סתר cether *say' -ther* or (fem.) סתרה cithrah which means secret, secretly, covert, secret place, hiding place, covering, disguise, privately, protection, to conceal, shelter.

When we first get saved, we hear so clearly from God. We dream dreams. We feel His anointing, Goose Bump City! It seems as if he hears our prayers so readily and answers them so quickly. We're prepared to take on giants bigger than Goliath. Then we pray and tell the Lord that we want to be closer to Him. Then **IT** happens! It seems like the last goose pimple you felt was when you stepped into a well air-conditioned house. You don't feel saved anymore. You're tempted with thoughts that you're backsliding, you've missed God. It seems as if you don't have the strength to turn over a page in your bible. And if we listen to these shouts from the enemy at the outer edge of God's darkness, we'll begin to stop doing the things we once did for Christ and miss a big blessing headed our way. The enemy knows that he can't touch you but he's hoping you will listen to your flesh and feelings to coax you out of the protective shadow of the almighty. If we understand this provision, we will not be taken by the enemy's attempts to prevent us from being blessed by God's provision.

### God's Darkness for the Believer

Here it's clear that the purpose of His secret place is for the good of those who serve Him and draw near into His pavilions of darkness. God also includes a certain nature of Himself with His pavilions of darkness, a secret place. Is it any wonder that what we pray in secret, God rewards openly? God is the master of covert operations and we are a part of it as we spend time in the secret place. He can carry out a plan with you right under the nose of the enemy. This secret place is just between you and the Lord, a place of total separation from any outside influence, any outside light. A hiding place is provided that we can be protected from the enemy and his devices. Jesus is our covering and He backs us up as we are obedient to His perfect will. In the Holy of Holies, there is no room for God's permissive will, but only His perfect will. A mature relationship with God will always choose the perfect will over permissive as a way of life because to whom much is given, much is required. God disguises us and shelters us when the enemy would like to destroy us. The secret place is a place of protection by concealment. The enemy can't reach you if he can't find you. And finally, the secret place is a shelter for all who will come under its roof.

As Psalms 91:1 mentions that the one that abides in the shadow of the almighty is the one that dwells in the secret place. The word **Dwelleth** ישׁב yashab (yaw-shab') means to sit, abide, inhabit, remain in, tarry, continue, place, still, to dwell. Obviously the secret place wasn't meant to be an occasional experience but rather a lifetime of existence. God doesn't desire to keep His people in the dark, rather he desires for us to draw close to Him and find that His darkness is full of light just as Israel received light from the darkness that held pharaoh's army back by the pillar of cloud and fire.

Being in God's pavilions of darkness isn't a place of exaltation but humility. Some experiences found in the secret place are when every prayer seems like stale toast and you're going through the motions, you haven't felt the spirit of God in a while and you begin to wonder if you've lost something in the Lord. Nothing could be further from the truth; you're in the pavilions of darkness. This is the place where God wants us to do what we know we should be doing by principle instead of by emotions or feelings.

When we seek to dwell in the secret place of God, he will help us with our own secret place of struggles to get things right in our lives. God's secret place is not comfortable to the soul or flesh. If we approach God, we will be faced with going through His pavilions of darkness round about Him. His darkness is a safe place of refuge.

This same darkness was upon the face of the earth.

*Ge 1:2   And the earth was without form, and void; and **darkness** (חשך choshek) was upon the face of the deep. And the Spirit of God moved upon the face of the waters.*

God used His darkness to hold the enemy of Israel from getting to them while God was delivering the Israelites across the Red Sea. God's darkness will be a light to us and God sees through the darkness as clearly as the day.

*Ex 14:20   And it came between the camp of the Egyptians and the camp of Israel; and it was a cloud and **darkness** (חשך choshek) to them, but it gave light by night to these: so that the one came not near the other all the night.*

*De 4:11   And ye came near and stood under the mountain; and the mountain burned with fire unto the midst of heaven, with **darkness** חשך choshek), clouds, and thick darkness.*

The darkness is a covering and a light for us.

*Ps 139:11   If I say, Surely the **darkness** (חשך choshek ) shall cover me; even the night shall be light about me. 12   Yea, the **darkness** (חשך choshek) hideth not from thee; but the night shineth as the day: the darkness and the light are both alike to thee.*

*Isa 45:3   And I will give thee the treasures of **darkness** (חשך choshek), and hidden riches of **secret places**, that thou mayest know that I, the LORD, which call thee by thy name, am the God of Israel.*

There are treasures to be had in the darkness of God. If we will abide, stay, and persist in God's darkness, we will receive treasures and riches in the secret place.

Jesus knew that the darkness is where he would speak to His people. Many preachers are receiving "real time" word behind the pulpit because they are before the congregation by principle and not out of emotion. Their steadfastness keeps them in the darkness where they can get the word for the day hot off the press! This is not to minimize the need for preparation rather that this is a result thereof.

*Mt 10:27  What I tell you in **darkness**, that speak ye in light: and what ye hear in the ear, that preach ye upon the housetops.*

Our enemies may try to rejoice when they see us in darkness but they don't realize that there is no safer place for us to be.

*Mic 7:8  Rejoice not against me, O mine enemy: when I fall, I shall arise; when I sit in **darkness** ( חשך choshek), the LORD shall be a light unto me.*

It's possible to obtain a level of brightness that your darkest day is as the noonday. In Isaiah 58:10, obscurity is the same Hebrew word for darkness.

*Isa 58:10  And if thou draw out thy soul to the hungry, and satisfy the afflicted soul; then shall thy light rise in **obscurity** ( חשך choshek), and thy darkness be as the noonday:*

It may seem contradictory that darkness will be our light, but remember that God separated the light from the darkness in Genesis 1. He knows how to see the light in darkness.

*Genesis 1:1  And God said, Let there be light: and there was light. 4  And God saw the light, that it was good: and God divided the light from the darkness ( חשך choshek). 5  And God called the light Day, and the darkness ( חשך choshek) he called Night. And the evening and the morning were the first day.*

Incidentally, the Hebrew word for Night is ליל layil *lah'-yil* which has one of the definitions of choshek; a protective shadow.

Surely Jesus' plan of dying on the cross was veiled in darkness/ or protected by a shadow. Had the enemy realized that crucifixion was the only way Jesus could fulfill the law, he would have never allowed Him to hang on that cross! Aren't you glad that God's plans aren't revealed for the enemy to see!

### God's Darkness for the Unbeliever

The day of the Lord is terrible to those who choose not to accept the Lord Jesus Christ. This same darkness has a tormenting side to those against Christ. God's enemies are pursued by His darkness! Is it any wonder why the wicked flee when no one is in pursuit (Proverbs 28:1)? This darkness is real and can be felt by God's enemies.

*Na 1:8   But with an overrunning flood he will make an utter end of the place thereof, and **darkness** ( חשך choshek) shall pursue his enemies.*

*Ex 10:21   ¶ And the LORD said unto Moses, Stretch out thine hand toward heaven, that there may be **darkness** ( חשך choshek) over the land of Egypt, even **darkness** ( חשך choshek) which may be felt.*

Praise God, can't you just see the Lord bringing Himself close to Egypt to over shadow it with one of His pavilions of darkness!

*Joe 2:31   The sun shall be turned into **darkness** ( חשך choshek) and the moon into blood, before the great and the terrible day of the LORD come.*
*Zep 1:15   That day is a day of wrath, a day of trouble and distress, a day of wasteness and desolation, a day of **darkness** ( חשך choshek) and gloominess, a day of clouds and thick darkness,*
*Am 5:20   Shall not the day of the LORD be **darkness** ( חשך choshek), and not light? even very dark, and no brightness in it?*

When the Lord uses His darkness, he draws Himself near to allow the pavilions of darkness round about Him to overshadow that which he desires to affect. When a saint draws himself into the darkness, it becomes a refuge, a light, a very present help. When the enemy is engulfed by the darkness of the Lord it is a place of torment, fear, woe, and misery. This is exciting to me because the enemy believes that he has the corner on the market of darkness. Don't tell him any different!

## ARK OF COVENANT & THE MERCY SEAT

*Exodus 25:10 ¶ And they shall make an ark [of] shittim wood: two cubits and a half [shall be] the length thereof, and a cubit and a half the breadth thereof, and a cubit and a half the height thereof. 11 And thou shalt overlay it with pure gold, within and without shalt thou overlay it, and shalt make upon it a crown of gold round about. 12 And thou shalt cast four rings of gold for it, and put [them] in the four corners thereof; and two rings [shall be] in the one side of it, and two rings in the other side of it. 13 And thou shalt make staves [of] shittim wood, and overlay them with gold. 14 And thou shalt put the staves into the rings by the sides of the ark, that the ark may be borne with them. 15 The staves shall be in the rings of the ark: they shall not be taken from it. 16 And thou shalt put into the ark the testimony which I shall give thee.*

*Ex 40:20 And he took and put the testimony into the ark, and set the staves on the ark, and put the mercy seat above upon the ark: 21 And he brought the ark into the tabernacle, and set up the vail of the covering, and covered the ark of the testimony; as the LORD commanded Moses.*

The Ark was the first piece of furniture that God gave instructions to be built. It was placed at the very head position of the cross. The order in which God instructed the building of the furniture was from His position towards man's position. He came down from His high position in the heavens so that he could commune with man. Consistently God has always made the first move to provide a way for man to have a relationship with Him.

## ARK OF COVENANT

Inside the Ark was placed an ephod of manna, the law brought down by Moses from Mount Sinai, and Aaron's rod that budded. Let's take a look at these items that were valued enough to be placed in the highest piece of furniture in the tabernacle.

### Manna

*Genesis 16:32 ¶ And Moses said, This is the thing which the LORD commandeth, Fill an omer of it to be kept for your generations; that they may see the bread wherewith I have fed you in the wilderness, when I brought you forth from the land of Egypt. 33 And Moses said unto Aaron, Take a pot, and put an omer full of manna therein, and lay it up before the LORD, to be kept for your generations. 34 As the LORD commanded Moses, so Aaron laid it up before the Testimony, to be kept.*

When the Lord brings us out of darkness and into His marvelous light, He wants to provide for us to get us to the next level. Not only does he want us to receive His provisions, he wants us to remember these provisions so that we can recall His love for us in times of trouble.

### Tables of Testimony (Ten Commandments or Law)

*Exodus 40:20 And he took and put the testimony into the ark, and set the staves on the ark, and put the mercy seat above upon the ark:*

It is so important for saints of God to keep the law before them that God saw fit to place it in the ark. This law was not meant to restrain them rather to liberate them. Understanding the Law enabled the people to know what they could and could not do. It's liberating to know the boundaries and it builds confidence in the people when they succeed in pleasing God. Confusion is a result of unclear boundaries and we know that God is not the author of confusion.

### Aaron's Rod that Budded

*Numbers 17: 5 And it shall come to pass, [that] the man's rod, whom I shall choose, shall blossom: and I will make to cease from me the murmurings of the children of Israel, whereby they murmur against you.*

**Figure 11. Ark of Covenant & Mercy Seat.**

*6 And Moses spake unto the children of Israel, and every one of their princes gave him a rod apiece, for each prince one, according to their fathers' houses, [even] twelve rods: and the rod of Aaron [was] among their rods. 7 And Moses laid up the rods before the LORD in the tabernacle of witness. 8 ¶ And it came to pass, that on the morrow Moses went into the tabernacle of witness; and, behold, the rod of Aaron for the house of Levi was budded, and brought forth buds, and bloomed blossoms, and yielded almonds. 9 And Moses brought out all the rods from before the LORD unto all the children of Israel: and they looked, and took every man his rod. 10 And the LORD said unto Moses, Bring Aaron's rod again before the testimony, to be kept for a token against the rebels; and thou shalt quite take away their murmurings from me, that they die not.*

Aaron's rod was representative of not only the tribe of Levites, but also the proof that God had chosen His headship. God does not ignore those who complain or murmur against His appointed leaders. God dealt harshly with Israel when they murmured against Moses. I believe the principle in 1 Chronicles 16:22 was in effect even though it had not been written yet:

**1Ch 16:22** *[Saying], Touch not mine anointed, and do my prophets no harm.*

All of the items placed in the ark of covenant were a memorial of God's provisions for the people in government (Ten Commandments or Law), food and His chosen leadership. The ark was not ready to support the Mercy seat until all the items for a testimony were placed inside. The Law is vital for the people to know the mind of God. Manna was provided to strengthen the people and demonstrate God's ability to be a leader and provider. The rod that budded was a memorial that God will back up those he has chosen as His leaders.

**MERCY SEAT**

*Exodus 25:17 And thou shalt make a mercy seat [of] pure gold: two cubits and a half [shall be] the length thereof, and a cubit and a half the breadth thereof.* **18** *And thou shalt make two cherubims [of] gold, [of] beaten work shalt thou make them, in the two ends of the mercy seat.* **19** *And make one cherub on the one end, and the other cherub on the other end: [even] of the mercy seat shall ye make the cherubims on the two ends thereof.* **20** *And the cherubims shall stretch forth [their] wings on high, covering the mercy seat with their wings, and their faces [shall look] one to another; toward the mercy seat shall the faces of the cherubims be.* **21** *And thou shalt put the mercy seat above upon the ark; and in the ark thou shalt put the testimony that I shall give thee.* **22** *And there I will meet with thee, and I will commune with thee from above the mercy seat, from between the two cherubims which [are] upon the ark of the testimony, of all [things] which I will give thee in commandment unto the children of Israel.*

The Mercy Seat was placed on the Ark of Covenant. Here, God said that he would dwell between the cherubim and meet with the High Priest. The Mercy Seat was the place to seek the mind of God.

Note that the Mercy Seat was the second piece of furniture to be made and also the first of two pieces that was a beaten work. Can you imagine the hours of labor put into beating this mass of pure gold into the form that God had designed? What a labor of Love.

Jesus is our mercy seat, and through the things he suffered, he provided a place for the presence of God to dwell and be among men, hence he was called Emmanuel which being interpreted is God with us.

### The Glory

The *Shekinah* and *Kabhode* glory resided and rested between the cherubim on the Mercy Seat.

### Shekinah – (*Sha Kahna*) *Glory*

The Shekinah glory is the symbol of the Divine presence that lead the Israelites from Egypt, and that finally rested over the ark in the tabernacle. This presence was visible to all of Israel as it funneled down from above the congregation to the Mercy Seat. It dwelt among the people of Israel as a manifestation of God's presence and leading. How comforting it must have been to look towards the tabernacle and see that the Lord is still among them.

### Kabhode – (*Kaw-Bode*) Glory

*Exodus 16:7 And in the morning, then ye shall see the **glory** of the LORD; for that he heareth your murmurings against the LORD: and what [are] we that ye murmur against us?*

The Hebrew definition for glory is כָּבוֹד kabowd (*kaw-bode'*) which is glory, honor, glorious, abundance, riches, splendor, dignity, reputation, and reverence.

*Romans 9:4 Who are Israelites; to whom [pertaineth] the adoption, and the **glory**, and the covenants, and the giving of the law, and the service [of God], and the promises;*

The Greek word for **glory** is δοξα doxa (*dox'-ah*) which is defined as glory, glorious, honor, praise, dignity, worship, majesty and splendor with brightness of the Sun, Moon and Stars.

Along with great responsibility, the mature ones in Christ also receive glory, honor, abundance, riches, splendor, dignity, reputation, and reverence. This is due to much being required to those who have been given much.

*Luke 12:48 But he that knew not, and did commit things worthy of stripes, shall be beaten with few [stripes]. For unto whomsoever much is given, of him shall be much required: and to whom men have committed much, of him they will ask the more.*

# 5

---

# THE CHRISTIAN'S JOURNEY

## (FROM BORN AGAIN TO FULL STATURE OF CHRIST)

*Corinthians 10:1 ¶ Moreover, brethren, I would not that ye should be ignorant, how that all our fathers were under the cloud, and all passed through the sea; 2 And were all baptized unto Moses in the cloud and in the sea; 3 And did all eat the same spiritual meat; 4 And did all drink the same spiritual drink: for they drank of that spiritual Rock that followed them: and that Rock was Christ.*

Israel's deliverance from the slavery and bondage of Egypt is parallel of a sinner receiving Christ into his heart. Egypt is a Type of the world and sin, and their journey from Egypt to Canaan's Land, is a picture of a Christian's journey from salvation to full spiritual maturity.

Entering into the courtyard of the Mosaic Tabernacle and moving into the Holy of Holies parallels this same concept of moving from salvation to spiritual maturity. Just as the High Priests worked from the Brazin Altar to the Ark and Mercy Seat, so also are we to work from the Brazin Altar to the Ark and Mercy Seat in the tabernacle in our hearts.

*1 Corinthians 3:16 ¶ Know ye not that ye are the temple of God, and [that] the Spirit of God dwelleth in you?*

*1 Corinthians 6:19* What? know ye not that your body is the temple of the Holy Ghost [which is] in you, which ye have of God, and ye are not your own?

We must learn to walk according to the principles laid out in the Mosaic Tabernacle to be truly successful in the Temple (Tabernacle) in our heart. To do that, God has some provisions and a purpose for us in Ephesians 4:11.

*Ephesians 4:11 And he gave some, **apostles; and some, prophets; and some, evangelists; and some, pastors and teachers**; 12 For the perfecting of the saints, for the work of the ministry, for the edifying of the body of Christ: 13 Till we all come in the unity of the faith, and of the knowledge of the Son of God, unto a perfect man, unto the **measure of the stature of the fulness of Christ**: 14 That we henceforth be no more children, tossed to and fro, and carried about with every wind of doctrine, by the sleight of men, and cunning craftiness, whereby they lie in wait to deceive; 15 But speaking the truth in love, may grow up into him in all things, which is the head, even Christ:*

God has provided apostles, prophets, evangelists, pastors and teachers to help us on our developmental journey with Him. His purpose is to get us to grow to the measure of the stature of the fullness of Christ. The tabernacle can be used as a measuring stick for our maturity level. With the Ark and Mercy Seat as the measure of the stature of the fullness of Christ, we can compare ourselves to the Tabernacle to see where we are and know where we want to grow. God never intended for His people to wonder around aimlessly without direction and purpose in their spiritual growth.

## (I.) The Courtyard experience.

*Hebrews 9:22 And almost all things are by the law **purged** with blood; and without shedding of blood is no remission.*

The Greek word for Purged is καθαριζω katharizo (*kath-ar-id'* –

*zo)* which means to cleanse, purify, remove stains, to be free from guilt of sin, to consecrate, dedicate, pronounce clean in a levitical sense. The root word katharos includes cleansing by fire.

With the Blood of Christ, our sins are forgiven. After forgiveness, the process of purging must take place in the heart. The Blood can purge almost all things. Some things in our hearts require the fire or the water to be purged. There are some things in our heart that need the purging power of fire and then the carrying away of the remains by the water.

The **Blood**, **Fire** and **Water** is the foundation of Christ and it is here in the first third of our journey where we will find the Doctrine of Christ in Hebrews 6:1–2 to be paramount to our spiritual foundation.

The frequency of the Blood, Fire and Water was at a minimum in the morning and evening daily by the priests in the Tabernacle. How much more should we offer up at minimum the Blood by asking for forgiveness, Fire by speaking in tongues and Water by reading the word to judge ourselves in the morning and evening on a daily basis?

The Mosaic Tabernacle was given to Israel once they entered into the wilderness. This would be the place that God would commune with man until the arrival of Jesus. The first two pieces of furniture ministered to before they entered into the Second of Three stages was the Brazen Altar and Brazen Laver. Between these two pieces, **Blood**, **Fire** and **Water** were administered. Jesus confirmed the necessity of the blood, fire and water to Nicodemus.

*John 3: 1 ¶ There was a man of the Pharisees, named Nicodemus, a ruler of the Jews: 2 The same came to Jesus by night, and said unto him, Rabbi, we know that thou art a teacher come from God: for no man can do these miracles that thou doest, except God be with him. 3 Jesus answered and said unto him, Verily, verily, I say unto thee, Except a man be **born again**, he cannot see the kingdom of God. 4 Nicodemus saith unto him, How can a man be born when he is old? Can he enter the second time into his mother's womb, and be born? 5 Jesus answered, Verily, verily, I say unto thee, Except a man be born of **water** and of the **Spirit**, he cannot enter into the kingdom of God. 6 That which is born of the flesh is flesh; and that which is born of the Spirit is spirit.*

To be **born again** is to receive Jesus into your heart (**Blood**). Once the blood has been applied, we are part of the family of God. However, God never intended for us to stop at the blood, he wants us to pursue the measure of the stature of Jesus Christ. To reach this high goal we must be born of **water** which is to be baptized in water (**Water**) and washed daily by the water of the word of God. Finally to be born of the **Spirit** is to be baptized with the Holy Ghost (**Fire**) daily burning.

Jesus is the same yesterday, today and forever. Israel's journey to Canaan's Land and the Priest's walk through the Mosaic Tabernacle support that the pattern for a healthy walk with God will consist of **Blood, Fire**, and **Water!**

*1 John 5:8 And there are three that bear witness in earth, the **Spirit**, and the **water**, and the **blood**: and these three agree in one.*

In the courtyard experience, judgement is necessary if we are to enter into the Holy Place expereince. No matter our position in the church, we must start at judgement each time we assend into the Holy Place.

Let us apply the Blood, Fire and Water in our lives twice a day at minimum as the priests did to assure that the Lord would speak to us, sanctify us and dwell among us. See Exodus 29:38-46.

### The Gift of the Blood (The first Brazin Altar experience)

When God created the heavens and the earth, he established many principles. The principle of sin and death was also established. To offset this principle, God also established that Life was in the Blood. After Adam and Eve's disobedience to God, they had placed themselves under the heavy weight of sin and death. God used the blood of innocent animals and provided coats of skin for their nakedness to offset the sin and death on their lives. Until the Christ was ready for His appearance, the blood of animals sufficed to allow man to have a relationship with God.

Jesus provided His blood as a gift which allows us to simply receive it. This gift is commonly known as the gift of salvation. Salvation is not based on feelings, emotions or circumstances, but by the word of God only.

God has made it clear what constitutes salvation in His word.

Receiving salvation, entering into the kingdom of heaven, receiving Christ in your heart, and being born again are synonymous. God's word is the measuring stick by which we will be judged on our salvation or lack thereof.

Jesus said:

*John 10:10 The thief cometh not, but for to steal, and to kill, and to destroy: I am come that they might have life, and that they might have it more abundantly.*

God doesn't take pleasure when something in our lives is stolen, killed or destroyed. He wants us to know that the enemy is the cause of these many forms of death. It's really simple; God is Love. There is Life here on earth and in eternity that can only come from Jesus. This life cannot be stolen, killed, or destroyed by the enemy.

*John 3:16 For God so loved the world, that he gave his only begotten Son, that whosoever* **believeth** *(πιστευω pisteuo) in him should not perish, but have everlasting life. 17 For God sent not his Son into the world to condemn the world; but that the world through him might be saved. 18 He that believeth on him is not condemned: but he that believeth not is condemned already, because he hath not believed in the name of the only begotten Son of God.*

The Greek word for Believeth is **πιστευω** pisteuo (*pist-yoo'o*); which means to commit to, commit to (one's) trust, be committed to, place confidence in, think to be true, and believer.

*Luke 19:10 For the Son of man (Jesus) is come to seek and to save that which was lost.*

*2 Peter 3:9 ¶ The Lord is not slack concerning his promise, as some men count slackness; but is longsuffering to us-ward, not willing that any should perish, but that all should come to repentance.*

It's clear that God's motive was to allow all of mankind to be saved. Some people believe that "they're too far gone to be saved". But God specializes in saving the lost and in His eyes you're either saved or lost.

The Greek word for Repentance is **μετανοια** metanoia (*met-an'-oy-ah*); which means a change of mind, to change one's mind for better, heartily to amend with abhorrence of one's past sins.

Once we repent we receive salvation, our past sins are amended with God.

**Here's how to receive salvation:**

**Romans 10:9** *That if thou shalt confess with thy mouth the Lord Jesus, and shalt believe in thine heart that God hath raised him from the dead, thou shalt be saved. 10 For with the heart man believeth unto righteousness; and with the mouth confession is made unto salvation. 11 For the scripture saith, Whosoever believeth on Him shall not be ashamed.*

Here's a prayer to help you receive Christ in your heart:

Say this prayer with your voice:

Lord Jesus I confess with my mouth that you are the Son of God and I believe in my heart that God has raised you from the dead. Forgive me of my sins. Come into my heart and be my Lord and Savior. I thank you for answering my prayer Lord. In Jesus' name I pray. Amen.

Congratulations!!! It's as simple as that. Welcome to the Kingdom of Heaven. Your Eternal Life starts now. You're part of the family of God, a Christian.

Remember!!!

**Romans 10:13** *For whosoever shall call upon the name of the Lord shall be saved.*

Even though we are saved, we still need to call upon the name of the Lord daily.

**Sin Offering**

I would like to emphasize that the sinless blood of Jesus brings the born again experience and causes the person to become a part of the body of Christ. This is the work of the sin offering that Jesus gave to the Father with His sin offering blood. Once an Israelite entered into the courtyard, they were required to bring a blood offering. Furthermore, when we receive Jesus' blood offering into our lives, we enter into the courtyard experience with Christ. In the Tabernacle, this was the most predominant offering and the blood was poured at the base of the Brazin Altar and on His horns. The blood would soak down to the depths of the soil to represent that no sin is too low that the blood can't reach. Horns speak of exaltation and defense showing that no sin is too high for His blood and that it will serve as a defense for those who use it. No one can be born again without the sin offering blood of Jesus Christ.

_**John 6:37**_ _All that the Father giveth me shall come to me; and him that cometh to me I will in no wise cast out._

### Whole Burnt Offering

There is a whole burnt offering portion of Jesus' blood in that he gave His destiny and life wholly into the hands of the Father so that we could use it for our whole burnt offering blood as the priests did in the Tabernacle. This offering was one of the three most predominant and was always answered by fire in the Tabernacle. A Christian who offers themselves as a whole burnt offering unto the Lord will most assuredly be answered by fire with the baptism of the Holy Ghost with the evidence of speaking in other tongues. This offering is an offering of oneself wholly unto the Lord to allow Him to dictate the relationship as he sees fit. This includes a mindset of letting Jesus Christ be Lord over our relationship and growth.

_**Romans 12:1**_ ¶ _I beseech you therefore, brethren, by the mercies of God, that ye present your bodies a living sacrifice, holy, acceptable unto God, [which is] your reasonable service._

Our reasonable service or the minimum requirements as a Christian is to offer ourselves to Christ as a living sacrifice. We do this when we present ourselves as a whole burnt offering unto the Lord and deny ourselves the right to disobey the word of God.

### Peace Offering

Jesus also gave a peace offering blood in that he was our sacrifice without spot or blemish because of His peace with the Father. The peace offering was the third of the three most predominant offerings made in the Mosaic Tabernacle. Many of us lack peace. God never designed our physical bodies to dwell without peace. Astonishingly, many Christians will have accepted the sin and whole burnt offerings and yet not be aware of the importance of the peace offering of our Lord Jesus. In the Old King James Version bible, there are four hundred entries of the word peace.

*John 14:27  **Peace** I leave with you, my **peace** I give unto you: not as the world giveth, give I unto you. Let not your heart be troubled, neither let it be afraid.*

*Colossians 3:15  And let the **peace** of God rule in your hearts, to the which also ye are called in one body; and be ye thankful.*

The Greek word for Peace is ειρηνη eirene (*i-ray'-nay)*. The definition speaks for itself in the many facets that peace applies:

1) a state of national tranquillity
1a) exemption from the rage and havoc of war
2) peace between individuals, i.e. harmony, concord
3) security, safety, prosperity, felicity, (because peace and harmony make and keep things safe and prosperous)
4) of the Messiah's peace
4a) the way that leads to peace (salvation)
5) of Christianity, the tranquil state of a soul assured of its salvation through Christ, and so fearing nothing from God and content with its earthly lot, of whatsoever sort that is
6) the blessed state of devout and upright men after death
This peace is indicative that there is no place for inward struggling.

When we find our hearts struggling, we must return to the peace offering and join ourselves to it.

How many times do we as Christians hang on to our sin offering blood and never move to the whole burnt blood and peace offering blood already provided. The sum of these three with the many blood provisions by Christ Jesus can change our countenance, our walk and our lives.

Let us move on unto even a higher level with Christ, the Fire.

## The Gift of the Fire (The second Brazin Altar experience)

John the Baptist was referring to Jesus when he said:

*Matthew 3:11 I indeed baptize you with water unto repentance: but he that cometh after me is mightier than I, whose shoes I am not worthy to bear: he shall baptize you with the Holy Ghost, and [with] fire:*

Jesus fulfilled this scripture on the day of Pentecost when the disciples were filled with the Holy Ghost and spoke in other tongues. The purpose of the Holy Ghost is to lead and guide us into all truth just as the Pillar of Cloud and Fire lead the Israelites from Egypt and Canaan's Land.

*John 16:13 Howbeit when he, the Spirit of truth, is come, he will guide you into all truth: for he shall not speak of himself; but whatsoever he shall hear, that shall he speak: and he will shew you things to come.*

Interestingly, Jesus could not have been speaking of the Spirit of God because the Spirit of God is ever present; he was referring to the Holy Ghost, which had not yet arrived. This fire is a gift from God. There is nothing we can do to earn it or deserve it. Jesus knows that we will need the fire to aid us in our wilderness experience. We can simply receive it regardless of our feelings because it is based on the word of God only and Jesus will never deny us that which we need to further our walk with Him. The fire experience is a gift freely given to all who seek it.

*Romans 11:29 For the gifts and calling of God [are] without repentance.*

God will never withdraw that which he has made a gift to all that come to Him. Let's take a look at how the Holy Ghost was introduced to the New Testament.

### Jesus Promised the Arrival of the Holy Ghost

*Acts 1:5 For John truly baptized with water; but ye shall be baptized with the Holy Ghost not many days hence. 8 But ye shall receive power, after that the Holy Ghost is come upon you: and ye shall be witnesses unto me both in Jerusalem, and in all Judea, and in Samaria, and unto the uttermost part of the earth.*

### The Promise Fulfilled

*Acts 2:2 And suddenly there came a sound from heaven as of a rushing mighty wind, and it filled all the house where they were sitting. 3 And there appeared unto them cloven tongues like as of fire, and it sat upon each of them. 4 And they were all filled with the Holy Ghost, and began to speak with other tongues, as the Spirit gave them utterance.*

### Two Examples of the Filling of the Holy Ghost

I chose these two examples to provide scriptural support that after the Blood has been received, the order of Fire and Water Baptisms is according to God's plan for you. Act 10: 44 shows that the people were baptized with the Holy Ghost before the water baptism. Acts 19:1 shows that people received water baptism before the baptism of the Holy Ghost. My point here is that the first requirement is that you receive Jesus into your heart first and then the order of fire and water is up to you and God.

*Acts 10:44 While Peter yet spake these words, the Holy Ghost fell on all them which heard the word. 45 And they of the circumcision which believed were astonished, as many as came with Peter, because that on the Gentiles also was poured out the gift of the Holy Ghost. 46 For they heard them speak with tongues, and magnify God. Then answered Peter, 47 Can any man forbid water, that these should not be baptized, which have received the Holy Ghost as well as we?*

***Acts 19:1*** *And it came to pass, that, while Apollos was at Corinth, Paul having passed through the upper coasts came to Ephesus: and finding certain disciples,* **2** *He said unto them, Have ye received the Holy Ghost since ye believed? And they said unto him, We have not so much as heard whether there be any Holy Ghost.* **3** *And he said unto them, Unto what then were ye baptized? And they said, Unto John's baptism.* **4** *Then said Paul, John verily baptized with the baptism of repentance, saying unto the people, that they should believe on him which should come after him, that is, on Christ Jesus.* **5** *When they heard [this], they were baptized in the name of the Lord Jesus.* **6** *And when Paul laid his hands upon them, the Holy Ghost came on them; and they spake with tongues, and prophesied.*

### The Purpose of Tongues

To understand the purpose of something is to know how to use it to its fullest potential without abusing it. The following is a list of purposes of tongues followed by the scriptures that back them up:

- To take on a new dimension of speaking to God.
- To speak mysteries.
- To edify oneself.
- To pray with the Spirit.
- To sing with the Spirit.
- To have the Spirit help our infirmities.
- To have the Spirit intercede for us according to the will of God.
- To build up ourselves on our most holy faith.

*1 Corinthians 14:2, 4, 14, and 15*
*2 For he that speaketh in an [unknown] tongue **speaketh not unto men, but unto God**: for no man understandeth [him]; howbeit in the spirit **he speaketh mysteries.** 4 He that speaketh in an [unknown] tongue **edifieth himself**; but he that prophesieth edifieth the church. 14 For if I pray in an [unknown] tongue, my spirit prayeth, but my understanding is unfruitful. 15 What is it then? **I will pray with the spirit**, and I will pray with the understanding also: **I will sing with the spirit**, and I will sing with the*

*understanding also.*

***Romans 8:26*** *Likewise the* **Spirit also helpeth our infirmities***: for we know not what we should pray for as we ought: but the Spirit itself maketh intercession for us with groanings which cannot be uttered.* ***vs. 27*** *And he that searcheth the hearts knoweth what [is] the mind of the Spirit, because he maketh* **intercession for the saints according to [the will of] God***.*

***Jude 1:20*** *But ye, beloved,* **building up yourselves** *on your most holy faith,* **praying in the Holy Ghost***,*

### Edification Principle

***1 Corinthians 14:4*** *He that speaketh in an [unknown] tongue edifieth himself; but he that prophesieth edifieth the church.*

It is impossible to edify others or the church if we are not edified. Therefore, interpreting this verse should include the importance of speaking in tongues as the foundation of prophecy. This dictates that one must speak in tongues before one can prophesy. Personally, I have never seen anyone prophecy that didn't speak in tongues.

### The Spirit Is Subject To You

***1 Corinthians 14:32*** *And the spirits of the prophets are subject to the prophets.*

Earlier it was established that speaking in tongues proceeded prophesying. With this rationale, if the spirit of the prophets is subject to the prophets, then speaking in another tongue is also subject unto us. Once you receive the Baptism of the Holy Ghost, it is up to you to use it. Just as you would turn on a faucet to get refreshed from the heat of the day, so also we can use the fire to refresh and revitalize our spirit. You are encouraged to use it whenever you can!

**The Power of Fire**

*Acts 1:8 But ye shall receive **power**, after that the Holy Ghost is come upon you: and ye shall be witnesses unto me both in Jerusalem, and in all Judaea, and in Samaria, and unto the uttermost part of the earth.*

Jesus told the disciples that they would receive power after the Holy Ghost had come upon them. This fire strengthened Peter to face a multitude concerning Christ when he could not face a few people around a fire earlier.

In this connotation, the Greek word for Power is δυναμιj dunamis (*doo' -nam-is*) which means power, mighty work, strength, miracle, might, virtue, mighty, and ability. It's worthy to note that the English word Dynamite comes from a derivative of dunamis. Further meanings are listed below:

    1a) inherent power, power residing in a thing by virtue of its nature, or which a person or thing exerts and puts forth
    1b) power for performing miracles
    1c) moral power and excellence of soul
    1d) the power and influence which belong to riches and wealth
    1e) power and resources arising from numbers
    1f) power consisting in or resting upon armies, forces, hosts

As we receive the Baptism of the Holy Ghost with the evidence of speaking in tongues, we will also receive power to be witnesses unto all nations. Just as the prophets of Baal were slain with the fire so we will slay the enemy's prophets with the power of speaking in other tongues.

**The Light of Fire**

It is no surprise to anyone that fire illuminates things around it. So as we continue in the Holy Ghost and speak in tongues, certain things that could not be seen in our heart are now visible. Some things we see are Godly and should encourage us. Some things are not godly and often hard to bear. We must walk with Jesus with an understanding that we cannot trust our own heart. When Jesus reveals things in our hearts, the only reply we can safely give is "yes Lord". After all, you can't clean a room in the dark!

*Jeremiah 17:9 The heart is deceitful above all things, and desperately wicked: who can know it?*

Jesus knows our hearts and he reveals negative things in us to allow us to repent or plead the blood that we can purge it out of our hearts. He not only does this as we pray and read the word of God with the Holy Ghost but also in our everyday living.

*Hebrews 4:12 For the word of God [is] quick, and powerful, and sharper than any two edged sword, piercing even to the dividing asunder of soul and spirit, and of the joints and marrow, and [is] a discerner of the thoughts and intents of the heart.*

When we visit the word of God, the Holy Ghost will point out our words, deeds, motives, and sins so that we can put them under the Blood and deny our flesh from these things. This is a way of life for the Christian and vital to ones spiritual growth.

Don't be down trodden or depressed that you see something in yourself that isn't Godly, rather ask Jesus to forgive you for what is in your heart and press on! Remember to welcome yourself to the human race! After all, that is why Jesus died on the cross, so that we can overcome our humanity.

## The Gift of Water (The Brazin Laver Experience)

To continue our spiritual growth, we must pursue baptism and daily washing of our hands and feet in the Word of God so that we can grow on unto perfection and move into the Holy Place. Just as the Brazin Laver was made of the looking glass of the women, at this level, the word is used as a mirror to show us ourselves that we may judge and purge our iniquities.

Let's take a look at what the word says about the water experience for Christians.

**Jesus led by example and was baptized.**

_Mat 3:16_ _And Jesus, when he was baptized, went up straightway out of the water: and, lo, the heavens were opened unto him, and he saw the Spirit of God descending like a dove, and lighting upon him:_

**Jesus gave the great commission to baptize.**

_Mat 28:19_ _Go ye therefore, and teach all nations, baptizing them in the name of the Father, and of the Son, and of the Holy Ghost:_

**Peter is the first to obey Christ's commission.**

_Acts 2:38_ _Then Peter said unto them, Repent, and be baptized every one of you in the name of Jesus Christ for the remission of sins, and ye shall receive the gift of the Holy Ghost._

**Being baptized is the answer of a good conscience.**

_1Peter 3:21_ _The like figure whereunto [even] baptism doth also now save us (not the putting away of the filth of the flesh, but the answer of a good conscience toward God,) by the resurrection of Jesus Christ:_

**Being baptized means to take on Jesus'' death and resurrection**

_Romans 6:4-8_
_**vs. 4** Therefore we are buried with him by baptism into death: that like as Christ was raised up from the dead by the glory of the Father, even so we also should walk in newness of life. **vs. 5** For if we have been planted together in the likeness of his death, we shall be also [in the likeness] of [his] resurrection: **vs. 6** Knowing this, that our old man is crucified with [him], that the body of sin might be destroyed, that henceforth we should not serve sin. **vs. 7** For he that is dead is freed from sin. **vs. 8** Now if we be dead with Christ, we believe that we shall also live with Him:_

**We are furthered in our attempt to be made conformable unto His death when we are baptized.**

*Philippians 3:10 That I may know him, and the power of his resurrection, and the fellowship of his sufferings, being made conformable unto his death;*

### Being baptized includes putting on Christ.

*Gal 3:27 For as many of you as have been baptized into Christ have put on Christ.*

We can see that baptism is vital to our walk with Jesus. Even as the priests went to the Brazin Laver, so we must be baptized and wash our hands (which speaks of our work) and feet (which speaks of our walk) daily before we can enter into a higher place with our Lord.

### Revelation of the Name of the Father, Son, and Holy Ghost

Being baptized in water is very important. If God went through painstaking details to furnish man an opportunity to have a relationship with Him, then how we are baptized should be as important as being baptized.

### God is Three AND One

I would like to point out that being baptized in the name of the Father, Son, and Holy Ghost or in Jesus' name has nothing to do with the trinity of God or the oneness of God. There are more scriptures supporting that God is three <u>and</u> one rather than God is three <u>or</u> one. Here are a few.

*Genesis 1:1 ¶ In the beginning **God** created the heaven and the earth.*

This reference to God is in the Hebrew language is אלדים 'elohiym (*el -o-heem'*) which is defined as a tri-une God. *Tri* to typify three and *une* to be defined unity or one.

*1 John 5:7 For there are three that bear record in heaven, the Father, the Word (Jesus), and the Holy Ghost: and these three are one.*

Finally, we were made in the image of God to include a Spirit, Soul, and Body. These three are one. We cannot explain fully how that we are three and one so let's not quibble on the subject of God being one or three. He's both!

## Should We Baptize in Jesus' Name?

There are three principles that support this study on Baptism in Jesus' Name. I will briefly cover these three principles and then cover them separately with scripture.

First, Jesus taught the disciples how to baptize in the Jordan river. Also, Jesus always spoke at the level of His audience. In Matthew 28:19, His audience consisted only of the eleven disciples, Jesus spoke to the disciples indirectly knowing he had taught them what the name of the Father, Son, and Holy Ghost was.

Secondly, obedience to God gets results! Obedience brings God's favor and support while disobedience brings a lack of God's favor and support. As we look at the way the disciples baptized and the results they achieved, we can conclude that they were obedient to Jesus' teaching on baptism.

Thirdly, baptism is the only outward demonstration that allows a believer to take on the name of the bridegroom and become named with the name of the whole family in heaven and earth; Lord Jesus Christ. Just as a bride proudly takes on the name of her groom, so the bride of the Lord Jesus Christ will proudly take on His name here on earth in baptism and in heaven.

Now let's take a closer look at these principles:

## The Lord taught the disciples how to baptize.

*John 4:1 ¶ When therefore the Lord knew how the Pharisees had heard that Jesus made and baptized more disciples than John, 2 (Though Jesus himself baptized not, but his disciples,)*

Here we can concede that Jesus would not have the disciples conduct a baptism incorrectly. So he supervised the practical training in the Jordan River. Jesus knew that the disciples had been taught correctly how to carry out His great commission. By us looking at how the disciples baptized and the results that were achieved, we can see more clearly how Jesus taught them to baptize.

*Mat 28:19 Go ye therefore, and teach all nations, baptizing them in the name of the Father, and of the Son, and of the Holy Ghost:*

Acts reveals that the disciples baptized in the name of the Lord Jesus Christ and the results were dynamic, showing clearly that they were obviously obedient to the instructions given in Mathew 28:19. If Jesus baptized in His name, then it begs the question; why didn't he just tell them to baptize in the name of the Lord Jesus Christ? My thought on this is that the humble man Jesus did nothing to lift His own name more than was necessary. Jesus always pointed people to the Father; this was easy because he was also called the everlasting Father in Isaiah 9:6. The disciples were clear on this principle when Jesus gave the great commission.

**Name of the Son is Lord Jesus Christ.**

*Acts 2:36 Therefore let all the house of Israel know assuredly, that God hath made that same **Jesus**, whom ye have crucified, both **Lord** and **Christ**.*

Jesus received the title and authority of Lord and Christ from the Father after he was crucified, spent three days and nights in hell and was resurrected by the Father. Therefore, His full name is Lord Jesus Christ.

**Name of the Holy Ghost is Lord Jesus Christ.**

Jesus said:

*John 14:26 But the Comforter, [which is] the Holy Ghost, **whom the Father will send in my name**, he shall teach you all things, and bring all things to your remembrance, whatsoever I have said unto you.*

Many believe that when the Father sends the Holy Ghost in Jesus' name that it means God sent Him in His authority. This is correct! In addition to authority, it also includes the literal name as well. Remember that God is multidimensional, so he has layers of revelation in the very word he speaks. In other words, he does and says things for many purposes to affect multiple causes. To nail God down to just two meanings of a scripture keeps God at our level. However for this study, we must understand that he not only sent the Holy Ghost in Jesus' Name but also in His authority and power.

**The Whole Family in Heaven and Earth is named Lord Jesus Christ.**

Paul had this revelation when he said:

**_Ephesians 3:14_** ¶ _For this cause I bow my knees unto the Father of our Lord Jesus Christ,_ **_15_** _Of whom the_ **_whole family in heaven and earth is named_**_,_

Not only is the Father, Son and Holy Ghost named Lord Jesus Christ, but the family of God on earth as well as in heaven. Taking on the name of the Lord Jesus Christ in baptism is simply the fulfillment of the literal side of the name and the beginning of a developmental process that changes ones nature into the nature of Christ. This is one reason that there is one name under heaven whereby we must be saved.

**Acts 4:12** Neither is there salvation in any other: for **there is none other name under heaven given among men, whereby we must be saved.**

**The Father's name is Lord Jesus Christ.**

It is true that the Father is the greatest of all fathers and that this connotes not only His loving nature as a father but also His position in the Godhead. His name and nature are synonymous. However, there is a name that sums up His love, deity, and Godhead. If the whole family in heaven and earth is named Lord Jesus Christ, then we can deduct that the Father's name is Lord Jesus Christ. Earlier we established that Isaiah 9:6 proclaimed that Jesus was the everlasting father. Therefore, Lord Jesus Christ is the Father's name and the Father was Lord Jesus Christ. It's no surprise when Jesus said that he and the Father are one.

**The apostles baptized in Jesus' Name.**

### Peter
*Acts 2:38 Then Peter said unto them, Repent, and **be baptized every one of you in the name of Jesus Christ** for the remission of sins, and ye shall receive the gift of the Holy Ghost.*

Peter not only directed them to be baptized in the name of Jesus, he promised results of receiving the Baptism of the Holy Ghost. He also proclaimed this doctrine before the other disciples and none corrected him, proving that they were in agreement.

### Peter and John
*Acts 8:14 ¶ Now when the apostles which were at Jerusalem heard that Samaria had received the word of God, they sent unto them Peter and John: 15 Who, when they were come down, prayed for them, that they might receive the Holy Ghost: 16 (For as yet he was fallen upon none of them: only they were **baptized in the name of the Lord Jesus**.) 17 Then laid they their hands on them, and they received the Holy Ghost.*

### Paul
*Acts 19:3 And he said unto them, Unto what then were ye baptized? And they said, Unto John's baptism. 4 Then said Paul, John verily baptized with the baptism of repentance, saying unto the people, that they should believe on him which should come after him, that is, on Christ Jesus. 5 When they heard [this], they were **baptized in the name of the Lord Jesus**.*

Here Paul's obedience to baptize as he was taught gained the result of them receiving the baptism of the Holy Ghost. Paul was baptized and taught by the other apostles. This supports my second principle that emphasizes that obedience gets results.

The Apostle's obedience was paramount for them to perform miracles through Jesus Christ. Therefore, baptism in Jesus Name is the answer to Jesus' commission and a sign of obedience.

_**Mat 28:19** Go ye therefore, and teach all nations, baptizing them in the name of the Father, and of the Son, and of the Holy Ghost:_

## A Bride always takes on the bridegroom's Name.

God has established that a bride would take on the name of her bridegroom at the altar. In fact, the bible doesn't record God ever calling Eve by her name. As a church, we are encouraged in the Word of God to grow to the measure and stature of Christ (Ephesians 4:13) that we may become the bride of Christ (this subject is covered more extensively in chapter 6). The bride of Christ will willingly take on the name of her bridegroom at the marriage supper. Water Baptism is the only ceremony that provides the process of taking on His name publicly here on earth.

If you have not been baptized in the name of the Lord Jesus Christ, your salvation is secure. However, if you are longing for more of Jesus, you will want to be baptized in the name of the Lord Jesus Christ as you seek your bridegroom.

Being baptized in the name of the Lord Jesus Christ is an experience that you'll never forget. You will go down in humility and be raised by the hand of God in exaltation!

I have been baptized twice, both in the name of the Lord Jesus Christ. I felt lead to openly testify of my desire to know Him more so I went down in the water on a second occasion. I'm staying open for another opportunity!

So far we have been focusing on two of the six principles of the doctrine of Christ recorded in Hebrews 6:1-2, repentance from dead works and the doctrine of baptisms. The courtyard is the place where all six principles are learned and established in a saint's life. These six foundational principles must be understood scripturally for a Christian to move into the Holy Place experience. I won't be covering these other principles very closely but I wanted to bring the scripture to light to give you an idea of what the six foundational truths of which I am referring.

_**Hebrews 6:1** ¶ Therefore leaving the principles of the doctrine of Christ, let us go on unto perfection; not laying again the foundation of **repentance from dead works**, and of **faith toward God**, 2 Of the **doctrine of baptisms**, and of **laying on of hands**, and of **resurrection of**_ *the dead, and of eternal judgment.*

Many Christians are entering into the Wilderness/Holy Place experience without the Fire and or the Water. Is it any wonder that some lose their joy, hope, and are brought back into captivity all because they did not go through complete judgment and separation. Not only is it important to follow the Spirit to allow God to deliver us from our old life, the Wilderness/Holy Place experience cannot be approached victoriously as the Lord would have it without the Blood, Fire and Water experience. Missing any of these components will cause a saint to be ill equipped in the Wilderness/Holy Place experience.

In the Wilderness/Holy Place experience, provided that we are innocent, when the Lord allows our enemies to move forward against us we must remember that it is simply a trap for them and deliverance for us.

## (II.) The Holy Place experience.

In the courtyard, a deliverance work was paramount. In the Holy Place, a development work is established. As we continue our walk with Jesus, we will experience diverse things that will bring the dross of our lives to the surface just as silver and gold is purified. With prayer and humility, we can allow each purifying stage to be a quick work.

*1 Corinthians 10: 5 but with many of them God was not well pleased: for they were overthrown in the wilderness. 6 ¶ Now these things were our examples, to the intent we should not lust after evil things, as they also lusted. 7 Neither be ye idolaters, as were some of them; as it is written, The people sat down to eat and drink, and rose up to play. 8 Neither let us commit fornication, as some of them committed, and fell in one day three and twenty thousand. 9 Neither let us tempt Christ, as some of them also tempted, and were destroyed of serpents. 10 Neither murmur ye, as some of them also murmured, and were destroyed of the destroyer. 11 Now all these things happened unto them for ensamples: and they are written for our admonition, upon whom the ends of the world are come. 12 Wherefore let him that thinketh he standeth take heed lest he fall.*

Verse 11 states that all these things were for an example of what to do and not to do. By looking at the results, it's plain that God didn't want Israel to murmur or complain. He wanted them to see the challenge before them, realize that they can't do it on their own and seek Him for the victory. In the Holy Place, our development comes with tribulations and trials to teach us the Lord's bidding concerning these issues. We will have similar trials as Israel did in the wilderness with money, fornication, murmuring and complaining, striving against headship, stubbornness, selfishness, lack of seeking God, presumption, the list goes on.

When Jesus said that he was the way, the truth and the life, He was implying that He was replacing the courtyard that would be the way, the Holy Place that would be the truth and the Holy of Holies that would be the life. When we receive Jesus in our heart, we have entered into the Way. As we deal with the truth about ourselves and the principles in the word of God, we enter into the truth. As we enter into the joy of living according to the word of God in maturity, we are able to enter into abundant life in the Holy of Holies. (See Figure 3)

As Israel journeyed through the wilderness, they were provided with prayer at the Golden Altar of Incense in the Holy Place to intercede for their concerns. They were provided light by the Golden Candlestick to understand how to walk according to God's word and finally they were provided bread at the Golden Table of Shewbread for strength to govern themselves accordingly. Jesus has empowered us to be the priest in the Holy Place, walking carefully and reverently before His throne.

## Prayer (The Golden Altar of Incense experience)

The wilderness of testing and trials is not the place for complaining, rather a place to fall on our knees and pray for God to intervene. I find it more than a coincidence that the Holy Place was the horizontal bar of the cross. Horizontal typifies humility, a place of falling on our faces before the Lord, prostrate, in our testing and trials. Clearly, the solution to the challenges we face is prayer. Naturally, when a saint crosses the threshold of the door of the tabernacle, the Golden Altar of Incense is found before them at the intersection of the cross. Prayer will always be at the heart of a saint's life. To give you an idea of the importance of prayer, as we journey to the Holy of Holies and back to the Brazen Altar, the Golden Altar of Incense is approached 6 times. The Ark of Covenant and Mercy

Seat are approached once and all other pieces of furniture twice. Let us set our hearts to approach the Holy of Holies on a daily basis.

When we consider prayer, we must ensure that listening is incorporated in the process. The Holy Place is a place of prayer and listening to the voice of the Lord. Is it any wonder that we can hear God's heart and will for our lives in the place that is located near the heart of the cross. I would like to encourage you to write what you hear at the altar of incense. These things that you record will confirm your faith in recognizing the Lord's voice.

*John 10:27 My sheep hear my voice, and I know them, and they follow me:*

Just as the heart supplies oxygen to the body, there are three pillars of prayer that supply strength to the body of Christ: Asking in Knowledge, Intercession, and Travail.

## Asking in Knowledge

Asking in knowledge is when we pray with our understanding. When we converse with the Lord on issues and seek His council and direction, we are asking in knowledge. To operate in the full potential, we must spend time quiet before the Lord that we can receive what the Lord has to say in response to our petition.

*1 Peter 3:12 For the eyes of the Lord [are] over the righteous, and his ears [are open] unto their prayers: but the face of the Lord [is] against them that do evil.*

*Matthew 7:7 ¶ Ask, and it shall be given you; seek, and ye shall find; knock, and it shall be opened unto you:*

*John 14:13 And whatsoever ye shall ask in my **name**, that will I do, that the Father may be glorified in the Son.*

God is not a spiritual bus boy waiting on us hand and foot. However, he has given us authority to ask according to His will for things that will further His kingdom.

In John 14:13 the Greek word for name is **ονομα** onoma (*on' -om-ah*) and is defined as the name used for everything which the name covers, the thought or feeling of which is aroused in the mind by mentioning, hearing, remembering, the name, i.e. for one's authority, interests, pleasure, command, deeds etc. When we ask in prayer according to His authority, interests, pleasure, commandments, and deeds we will most assuredly get results. To perfect our ability to pray according to Jesus' will, we can ask a very simple question: What would Jesus do?

## Intercession

**Romans 8:26** ¶ Likewise the Spirit also helpeth our infirmities: for we know not what we should pray for as we ought: but the Spirit itself maketh intercession for us with groanings which cannot be uttered.

When we operate as intercessors, we will find ourselves moving from intelligible words to groans that seek the Lord to move on the behalf of someone or something other than ourselves. The purpose for Intercession is to pray for others. Many parents and grandparents spend time in intercession for their children. Intercession can take on the form of stammering lips and another tongue as the Spirit of the Lord speaks through us.

Jesus is our intercessor to the Father.

***Romans 8:34*** *Who [is] he that condemneth? [It is] Christ that died, yea rather, that is risen again, who is even at the right hand of God, who also maketh intercession for us.*

Intercession in Greek is **εντυγχανω** entugchano (*en-toong-khan' – o*) not only means to pray and entreat but also to go to or meet a person, esp. for the purpose of conversation, consultation, or supplication. This brings a deeper cause for intercession that we can enter into a conversation, seek consultation, or supplicate our cares to the Lord.

When Jesus makes intercession for us to the Father, he does so at the Golden Altar of Incense in the tabernacle in heaven.

**Travail**

*Galatians 4:19 ¶ My little children, of whom I travail in birth again until Christ be formed in you,*

The Greek reference for travail in birth is ωδινω odino (*o-dee' –no*). This phrase is given to pains of child birth.

Nothing can be brought into birth of the Lord without travail. Travail can take on the form of pangs as a saint prays earnestly before the Lord for a ministry or a new work of God. This application can be at a personal level or a ministry level.

The root word for odino is ωδιν odin (*o-deen*)'. Odin includes the pains of child birth and adds intolerable anguish; in reference to the dire calamities that preceded the advent of the Messiah.

The Hebrew word for Travail is תלאה t@la'ah (*tel-aw-aw'*) which implies trouble, toil, hardship, distress, weariness

When we find ourselves in distress or intolerable anguish, we must approach the Golden altar of incense and travail into birth a greater portion of the Messiah in our situations, lives and others.

When Jacob was about to reunite with his brother Esau, Genesis 32 reveals that he was afraid and distressed. Verse 24 states that he was left alone and wrestled with a man until the breaking of the day. Jacob's name was changed to Israel and he said that he had seen God face to face. Travail doesn't bring a birth without the tenacity to disregard personal imposition and pain. The rewards are tremendous to those who persevere.

**Studying the Word of God (The Golden Candlestick experience)**

Up to this point, the word has been used to judge our sins that we may draw closer to God. However, at this stage, the purpose of the word is to light our path, help us learn more about the principles of God, a place to receive revelations and give us direction. Wisdom, understanding, knowledge and prudence are obtained here. Normally Wisdom, Understanding, and Knowledge are often interchanged synonymously because their definitions usually include each other. However, for the sake of increasing our revelation of a difference, I want to define their differences in ascending order.

## Wisdom

Wisdom is like the olive oil that burned in the Golden Candlestick. The olive tree has the wisdom to be the first to bloom at the command of springtime. This oil comes from a tree of immediate obedience. We must learn to be quick about our obedience like the olive tree. At the very hint of His desire of us, we must rush to satisfy our Lord.

*Proverbs 4:7 Wisdom [is] the principal thing; [therefore] get wisdom: and with all thy getting get understanding.*

The Hebrew word for Wisdom is חכמה chokmah (*khok-maw'*) and comes from the root word חכם chakam (*khaw-kam'*). These words bring the connotation of being able to recognize and having a humble heart to receive wisdom. Not only the ability to be made wise but also the ability to share, teach, and make others wise.

Wisdom is the principle thing as a foundation is to a building. The first thing done when a new building is being conceived is the recognition of the potential of the magnitude of the building that can be put in place. Then the foundation is poured in depth, width and breadth that would accommodate the building it is to support. And so the Hebrew word for Principle is ראשית re'shiyth (*ray-sheeth'*) defined as first, beginning, best, chief and choice part. Wisdom is our foundation to understanding, knowledge and prudence. It is the insight or perception of a principle that exists. Without wisdom, there can be no understanding, knowledge and prudence.

The deeper the foundation, the higher the building to be built. We needn't be afraid of the depth of our foundation, only encouraged by the heights to come!

Wisdom is being aware or cognizant of a spiritual principle.

## Understanding

Understanding is like the fire that burns the oil in the Golden Candlestick, the heat contributes to the process of consuming the oil of wisdom. In order to allow a principle to work on our behalf, we must add understanding of the specific rules or laws that govern the principle.

***Proverbs 3:13*** ¶ *Happy [is] the man [that] findeth wisdom, and the man [that] getteth* **understanding***.*

The Hebrew word for Understanding is תבון tabuwn (*taw-boon'*) and (fem.) תבונה t@buwnah (*teb-oo-naw'*). Each comes from the root word בין biyn *bene*. These words bring the intellect into the picture with having the faculty to reason with the laws of a given principle, discretion, the object of knowledge and finally the ability to teach what is understood. This is the point where we understand how to apply the principles or wisdom without actually applying them yet; we have the concept through wisdom and the way to applying it through understanding.

Notice that wisdom is something that can be found. The implication here is that one must be actively searching for the location of wisdom. Understanding is gotten, implying that understanding can be received by going to a known destination. Both require a proactive assertion on the part of the recipient. Once wisdom is found, the location of understanding is not far.

Again, understanding is being aware or cognizant of how to apply the principle that you have obtained by wisdom; I call this "Theoretical".

## Knowledge

Knowledge is the light produced by the Golden Candlestick. The oil of wisdom and the fire of understanding combine to produce light that the Holy Place would be illuminated. It isn't until the fire is combined with oil that the light of knowledge is obtained. It isn't until the theory is put into practice that Knowledge is achieved to bring a new thing to birth. Adam knew Eve and she conceived so also when the theoretical is coupled to empirical, new things will always bring to birth

The priests could conduct their daily duties because the Candlestick was never allowed to be extinguished. So also is the Word of God today, still shining bright to all those will embrace it.

***Proverbs 2:6*** *For the LORD giveth wisdom: out of his mouth [cometh] knowledge and understanding.*

The Hebrew word for Knowledge is דַּעַת da'ath (*dah'-ath*) and comes from the root word יָדַע yada' (*yaw-dah*). These words include both wisdom and understanding as part of their definition with the addition of discernment, perception and skill. When we put a principle to practice in our lives, regardless of our experience level, our knowledge, perception, skill, discernment, understanding and wisdom will be sharpened in that area. This brings to light the importance of James 1:22 and Hebrews 5:14.

**James 1:22** *But be ye doers of the word, and not hearers only, deceiving your own selves.*

Having a theoretical capacity is simply the first stage (wisdom & understanding). Putting what we know into action gives us the practical or empirical knowledge into that which that the Lord would have us to ascend. Please don't misunderstand, we all must sit and be taught, however, some lessons from God can only be received by doing rather than just hearing.

**Hebrews 5:14** *But strong meat belongeth to them that are of full age, even those who by reason of use have their senses exercised to discern both good and evil.*

We can only exercise our senses by doing the word. There is no other way! There must be a point in our walk with Christ that becomes clear to us that we can grow no further unless we begin to apply the word practically in our lives. It is when we do the word that we see new things birthed into our lives. After all, Adam knew Eve and she conceived and birthed his sons. To know a principle is to bring forth a birth between theoretical and empirical experiences.

Knowledge is putting into practice the wisdom and understanding that you have gained. Just do it!

**Prudence**

Prudence is the greatest among wisdom, understanding and knowledge because it is the mindset that comes back to the foot of the cross as if it were the first time. Prudence is founded by humility in that we choose to humble ourselves with all the wisdom, understanding and knowledge we have gained thus far. God is unlimited in what he can teach us, therefore, we should pursue prudence and joyfully choose the low place even if we have obtained great revelation.

**Proverbs 12:23** *A **prudent** man concealeth knowledge: but the heart of fools proclaimeth foolishness.*

Prudence is defined by עָרְמָה 'ormah *(or-maw')* wilily, subtilty, wisdom, shrewdness, and craftiness. Being prudent is better described in Matthew 10:16.

**Matthew 10:16** *Behold, I send you forth as sheep in the midst of wolves: be ye therefore wise as serpents, and harmless as doves.*

A prudent man knows that the knowledge he has is primarily for him and subject to the leadership of the Holy Ghost for others. He must protect that which has been bestowed upon him. That is to say, not everyone wants to hear what we know. Many people attain such a great height of knowledge and never address prudence in their lives so they become a stench to others. Having great knowledge in the Word of God and lack prudence is like salt with no savor. Prudence chooses humility at times of temptation when the flesh would like nothing better than to have its way and tell them who their messing with.

**Wisdom, Understanding, Knowledge and Prudence**

Gravity is a principle; a principle is an undisputable law which is unbiased and impartial. If we violate it, it will hurt us. If we work with it, comply with its laws, it will help us. Using the Wisdom, Understanding, Knowledge and Prudence approach to gravity: the wisdom of gravity is having the realization of its existence. Understanding is the ability to comprehend the laws by which gravity operates and an idea of how to work with it. Wisdom and Understanding operate under theoretical comprehension (theoretical knowledge if you will). Knowledge is the marriage of wisdom and understanding with practical experience or applying what you understand. Knowledge brings to birth a new light on the subject as we put to practice the Wisdom and Understanding we have received, which causes Knowledge to fall under the empirical experience (empirical knowledge). Prudence is the final stage of this process in that theoretical and empirical knowledge are still not complete until we gain the prudence to know that we have something special from God and still choose to sit and submit to be taught more wisdom. Prudence is the ability to choose the humble place of submission with the awareness of the things that God has given us.

**Governing oneself according to the Word of God (Golden Table of Shewbread experience).**

As we leave the Golden Candlestick experience, we are once again confronted with the Golden Altar of Incense before continuing to the Golden Table of Shewbread experience. Prayer to absorb the word that we have received from the Candlestick is vital to our next stage, for the Golden Table of Shewbread experience is indicative of action. This bread is used for strengthening us so we may govern ourselves or act according to the word we received from the Golden Candle Stick. Just as the Golden Candlestick is a lamp unto our feet and light unto our path (Psalms 119:105), so is the Golden Table of Shewbread the provision for walking accordingly to this lamp and light.

It bears repeating that Jesus said;

*John 4:34* *Jesus saith unto them, My meat is to do the will of him that sent me, and to finish his work.*

It's no coincidence that the meat offering given by the people of Israel for the Table of Shewbread was for strength to perform the priestly duties. Jesus defined the new covenant meat offering that we give unto the Lord as doing His will. Many are thwarted here because they are convinced that the meat of the word is a deeper revelation. To some degree, this is true. The means by which we get this deeper revelation is through working the word. A certain level of understanding in the word can only be obtained by laboring in the ministry in some form. Many corporations understand that application of knowledge is more valuable than knowledge alone. Most businesses incorporate what is known as "on the job training" to bring employees to this level of knowledge. Surely by now you recognize that this is a principle that the Lord has established. We must apply ourselves to "on the job training" with working the word.

Our meat is to do the will of Jesus. What Jesus saw the Father do, He also did. Likewise, we are to follow Jesus in that what we see Jesus do, we are to do. As we eat of the portion of the word that will strengthen us to do that which we see, we will have increased our faith and revelation in the word. This is how God works his will into us.

*Philippians 2:13 For it is God which worketh in you both to will and to do of [his] good pleasure.*

There is sustaining power in our lives when we combine the wisdom and understanding of the word with action. This marriage is the knowledge that brings forth new life and strength to those whose operate under this principle.

**Meat in my house.**

The necessity of keeping meat in the house of God was not only for the priests but also for the people who gave. What we do and give in the house of the Lord will not only strengthen us but also bless us. Obedience is a powerful tool in our hands!

*Malachi 3:10 Bring ye all the tithes into the storehouse, that there may be **meat** in mine house, and prove me now herewith, saith the LORD of hosts, if I will not open you the windows of heaven, and pour you out a blessing, that [there shall] not [be room] enough [to receive it].*

To give your life at this stage is to give of your time, talents, gifts, possessions, and money to the Lord's work. Just like all the positions in the tabernacle, you don't have to be a spiritual giant to practice or experience this stage. Young or old in the Lord, we can start at our level of faith and allow God to bring us higher in capabilities. Doing the work of the Lord in any capacity (cleaning churches, greeters, sound ministry, administration, etc) is a dynamic way for the Lord to increase your depth in the word and strengthen you to carry on throughout the week. We will reap what we sow, if we need strength, then we must sow strength in His work. Truly our meat will be doing the will of Jesus.

It is tragic to see christians who are weak and don't know that God has a table of provisions for them to be strengthened and increased in faith. When we eat of the governmental loaves of faith, we are strengthened that we faint not!

*Galatians 6:9* *And let us not be weary in well doing: for in due season we shall reap, if we faint not.*

Finally, I would like to point out that before one can crawl under the veil to stand before the glory of the Lord in the Holy of Holies, a work must have been done in the courtyard first and then the Holy Place.

**Looking into Canaan's Land**

When we see our Canaan's land or the promise that God has given us for the first time, we may be tempted to shrink back at the great challenges set before us. The giants in the land may be a little intimidating and we may lose sight of what the Lord has done for us thus far. We may even consider returning to our old life but let us *"Trust in the LORD with all our heart; and lean not unto our own understanding" (Proverbs 3:5)* and press towards the presence of God to get His leadership on the matter. The miracle is that God brings us through so many deliverances to assure us that He will be with us through this as well. We achieve the unthinkable when we shift the focus from our abilities to God's.

The same is true when we find ourselves on our knees looking into the glory of the Lord in our Holy Place. Our first inclination might be to back out. But if we move forward to stand before His awesome presence, we will know life like no other!

**(III.) The Holy of Holies experience.**

Here the full measure and stature of Jesus Christ is found as stated in Ephesians 4:13. We are to grow into a mature bride. His bride is accustomed to the Holy of Holies. She longs to look into the face of her bridegroom. Her mentality is as Christ's to include saying in her heart "Lord, forgive them, for they know not what they do". She willingly gives her sacrifice of Love for her bridegroom. The wounds she has received is only for a better reward from her Lord. She is selfless and unconcerned with anything other than pleasing Jesus. She follows Him in the chasm of His darkness willingly and is comfortable with trusting His leading completely. Her hidden agendas have long been abandoned and come what may, she is willing to accept His will for her life,

*Ephesians 4:13   Till we all come in the unity of the faith, and of the knowledge of the Son of God, unto a perfect man, **unto the measure of the stature of the fulness of Christ:***

When God started to instruct Moses to build the Tabernacle, He began where He is, the Holy of Holies, and moved towards the Brazin Altar in the courtyard. In order to accomplish this, the Lord had to restrict His glory exponentially every step he made towards man. You see, every time the glory is reduced, liberty is reduced. Inversely, when we step higher in the Lord, we find ourselves exponentially in greater glory and liberty. At the Holy of Holies, this liberty sees the way God sees, feels the way God feels, has His compassion, mercy, grace and patience. When the bride chooses to submit to the word continually, her spiritual stature does not inhibit her from seeking the Lord with great humility. In balance, she approaches the Lord with a maturity like a natural bride walks down the aisle at the wedding. She plays before the Lord but doesn't play with the Lord. Her concern is that she continually finds favor in her Lord's eyes.

The Holy of Holies has many revelations, mindsets and principles working in our lives as Christians. However the limitation of this book will only allow me to cover just a few.

### The Pulpit

In the house of God, the pulpit sits at the same place as the Ark of Covenant and Mercy Seat. It's common for the man of God to prepare for the service and still not see God's plan until he steps behind the pulpit. In the darkness, the preacher stands before the Lord with his hand out waiting for the Lord to place something in his heart. Once in his heart, the preacher can then pass it on to the people. In the darkness, the preacher may not feel the anointing but the results are miraculous! A mature relationship with Christ doesn't walk by feelings and emotions, rather by principles established by the word of God and faith.

Also, the funnel of the pillar of cloud and fire that mushroomed down and rested between the cherubim on the Mercy Seat now rests on the pulpit. The pulpit is a place of power, healing, deliverance, reconciliation, adoption, mercy, judgment, the mind of God, and is the equivalent of the Holy of Holies. Hence the pulpit must be set aside and revered as the most holy place in the church.

## Understanding Your Anointing

Incidentally, when mature Christian's walk with Christ, they understand that their anointing isn't for them, but for those who they must minister. They don't rely on feeling their anointing as they perform their duties, but concentrate on following the principles that they have been taught by the Lord. They know that it's common to feel other's anointing before they feel their own.

## Choosing to Increase in Knowledge

In whatever state the bride finds herself, she never overlooks the fact that she is in need of more wisdom, understanding, knowledge and prudence of principles she is unaware. She knows that a principle is a law that cannot be debated. Just as gravity, if she works with it, it will help her. If she violates it, it will hurt her. Many other principles in the word of God operate in the same manner. How many times do we violate a principle that we are unaware due to lack of studying the Word of God? The Word of God has provisions for ignorance so we can pray "Lord, forgive me of my sins, known and unknown."

## Called, Chosen and Faithful

*Matthew 22:14 For many are **called**, but few [are] **chosen**.*

***Revelation 17:14*** ¶ *These shall make war with the Lamb, and the Lamb shall overcome them: for he is Lord of lords, and King of kings: and they that are with him [are]* **called, and chosen, and faithful**.

We all have a calling to salvation. The measure of our heart's willingness to submit to the Lord Jesus Christ will qualify us to be chosen. As Revelations 17:14 clearly states, they that are with Him at this great battle are called, chosen and faithful. If we want to be with Him, then we must submit to Him faithfully. Faithfulness is the greater attribute of the three because it requires accountability, responsibility and consistency. Jesus is faithful to His bride and expects the same from her. His bride will be faithful in heart, deeds and consistency in all. She pursues Him and he pursues her, this is a mature relationship. For Love is not a feeling, but a commitment!

# 6

---

---

# *GLORY REWARDS*
# *FOR*
# *GROWTH*

## *WHY IS THIS IMPORTANT?*

I was asked this question by a truly sincere Christian. I think she was saying: *Shouldn't our focus and motivation be centered on our relationship with Jesus rather than what we can get out of it?* My response is a resounding ABSOLUTELY! In addition to that, I should be willing to learn whatever I can in the Word of God...after all; He put the rewards in the bible for a reason. Jesus is the Word as stated in John chapter 1 so I would be remiss to omit a portion of Jesus or His word just because it covers my rewards for the maturity I achieve on this earth. I would like to think that for some, this revelation will inspire them to do more for Christ and their maturity.

*Mt 11:28 Come unto me, all [ye] that labour and are heavy laden, and I will give you rest. 29 Take my yoke upon you, and learn of me; for I am meek and lowly in heart: and ye shall find rest unto your souls. 30 For my yoke [is] easy, and my burden is light.*

Verse 29 implies that as I learn of him, I gain rest unto my soul. I can't help but wonder what portion of rest I forfeit if I avoid studying any subject of Him.

With that said, let's explore the subject of Glory Rewards for Growth:

***Hebrews 6:1*** *¶ Therefore leaving the principles of the doctrine of Christ, let us go on unto perfection; not laying again the foundation of repentance from dead works, and of faith toward God,  2 Of the doctrine of baptisms, and of laying on of hands, and of **resurrection of the dead**, and of **eternal judgment**.*

Eternal Judgment will not only sentence each one of us to Heaven or Hell, but also reward the righteous in commensurate to their growth and works on earth.

***1Corinthians 15: 41*** *There is one glory of the sun, and another glory of the moon, and another glory of the stars: for one star differeth from another star in glory.  **42 So also is the resurrection of the dead** . . .*

Jesus gave many parables of the kingdom of heaven to teach us what heaven is like. In Matthew 25:14-30, Jesus tells the parable of a man who leaves his country and leaves his three servants in charge of some talents in his absence. He starts the parable with "The Kingdom of heaven is like" Upon the master's return; the servants were required to give an account of their assignment. Two of the servants had pleased the master by taking their talents and bringing an increase to the Master, but the third was accused of being wicked and slothful because there wasn't an increase, so he was cast into outer darkness.

God has an assignment for each and every one of us and he has given us the talent to carry it out. On the Day of Judgment, we will be held accountable to show an increase in our lives. If you don't know what your assignment is, I can tell you that it will always be a facet of praising and giving glory to God and will never include sin (sin is anything that is contrary to the word of God). I have an associate that goes drinking at the bar. He tells me that he speaks to them about God as if this was his calling. I can assure you that God takes no pleasure in poor examples for a witness. Jesus led by example so that we could lead by example. I'm not saying that you should not go to a bar to witness, I'm saying that if you are engaging in worldly activities then there won't be any anointed drawing power when you speak.

One talent God has given you is your life. If you hide your life in a hole to return it back to God without an increase in spiritual maturity, you are in danger of becoming just like the third servant who was cast into outer darkness. Let the Lord teach you how to grow in Him and you will prosper in your spirit, soul, and body!

## The Invisible is seen by the Visible

*Romans 1:20  For the invisible things of him from the creation of the world are clearly seen, being understood by the things that are made, [even] his eternal power and Godhead; so that they are without excuse:*

We can see the invisible things of God from the visible things God has created. The Word of God points our attention to specific things to lead us into the direction God wants us to concentrate. If we haven't taken a close look at what God has pointed out to us, then we need to put down the other things until we learn what the Father is trying to teach us for our best interests. For example, the sun, moon, and stars reflect God's eternal power and Godhead.

## Sun, Moon and Star glory

*1Corinthians 15: 41 There is one glory of the sun, and another glory of the moon, and another glory of the stars: for one star differeth from another star in glory.  42 SO ALSO IS THE RESURRECTION OF THE DEAD. It is sown in corruption; it is raised in incorruption:  44 It is sown a natural body; it is raised a spiritual body. There is a natural body, and there is a spiritual body.*

The bible records different levels of heaven and hell. However, my objective will be to cover the different levels of Heaven because the best level of Hell is more torment than anyone would want to endure. So let's look at the degrees of rewards in heaven!

Regardless of the glory that you will receive after the judgment, it will be according to the spiritual growth you obtained in your natural body. To put it another way, the maturity level we attain in this life will be directly proportional to the reward in heaven. Hence the latter portion of verse 42: "It is sown in corruption; it is raised in incorruption". Verse 44 puts it more clearly that our works are seeds sown here on earth in our natural body and raised in a spiritual body. Another reference to the sun, moon, and stars comes in the form of New Jerusalem, New Earth, and New Heaven respectively in Revelation 21:1.

*Revelation 21:1 ¶ And I saw a **new heaven** and a **new earth**: for the first heaven and the first earth were passed away; and there was no more sea. 2 And I John saw the holy city, **new Jerusalem**, coming down from God out of heaven, prepared as a bride adorned for her husband.*

## Star Glory (New Heaven)

The correlation of the star glory with the new heaven is an easy one to see. On a clear night we can look into the heavens and notice that some stars have more glory, or brilliance, than others do because of the varying distances. Hence one star is different than another star in glory. The new heaven will be filled with a new type of heavenly bodies; the righteous that obtained star glory during their walk here on earth.

## Moon Glory (New Earth)

The correlation of the glory of the moon with the new earth can be better understood with pictures taken of the earth by the astronauts while standing on the moon. In retrospect of their position with the sun, the glory of the moon and the glory of the earth are basically the same. The difference between the earth and the moon is that 360 degrees of the earth's surface experiences day and night time while the moon only experiences day time on approximately 210 degrees of the its surface. Because the earth has a better balance of both day and night time, it is understandable that the New Earth would be identified in Revelation 21:1 and 7:15 instead of the moon.

***Revelation 7:15*** *Therefore are they before the throne of God, and serve him **day and night** in his temple: and he that sitteth on the throne shall dwell among them.*

It should be clear that those who obtain the New Earth glory are brighter than those who obtain the star glory. In the evening, when the full moon is out, the moon's glory outshines that of any star(s) near it. With the right conditions, the stars actually disappear before the moon hides them by its body, in essence swallowing up, the stars and their glory.

I would like to point out that this spiritual reward, the New Earth, has a day and night season. The New City doesn't have a night season, implying that the New City is located elsewhere.

## Sun Glory (New City)

***Revelation 21:9*** ¶ *And there came unto me one of the seven angels which had the seven vials full of the seven last plagues, and talked with me, saying, Come hither, I will shew thee the **bride**, the Lamb's wife. **10** And he carried me away in the spirit to a great and high mountain, and shewed me that **great city, the holy Jerusalem**, descending out of heaven from God,*

***Revelation 21:22*** *And I saw **no temple therein**: for the Lord God Almighty and the Lamb are the temple of it. **23** And the city had no need of the sun, neither of the moon, to shine in it: for the glory of God did lighten it, and the Lamb is the light thereof. **24** And the nations of them which are saved shall walk in the light of it: and the kings of the earth do bring their glory and honour into it. **25** And the gates of it shall not be shut at all by day: for **there shall be no night there**.*

If there ever was a doubt of the position of the bride, Revelation 21:9-10 confirms that the New City and the bride are one and the same. The remainder of chapter 21 describes the New City with its splendor. Verse 22 points out that no temple was needed because Jesus is the temple. This Holy City is described as never having a night season because the Lord is its continual light. This perspective can only be from a position of constant light, a *sun* perhaps.

When we look at our daytime and nighttime, we can get a revelation of what some of the characteristics the different glories in heaven possess. When the sun is out, the stars are engulfed by the sun's glory and as long as the moon doesn't get too close to the sun, one can see the moon during the day. On a clear night as we watch the moon, any stars close to the moon comes close to are engulfed by the glory or brightness. So it is safe to say that the glory of the sun is greater than the moon's and the glory of the moon is greater than the stars.

God's eternal Godhead deals with, but is not limited to, the final arrangement after the complete fulfillment of the scriptures. So those with the glory of stars will be placed in the new heavens. Those with the glory of the moon will be placed in the new earth. And those with the glory of the Sun will find themselves in the New City.

**To Whom is which glory given?**

To answer this question clearly, we must go back to the principles taught in the earlier chapters. The parallelism of Israel's journey and the spiritual journey of a Christian can help us see how and where the rewards are placed. Here the spiritual rewards can be easily applied to the three major parts of the Israel's journey, the tabernacle and the Christian's spiritual growth. (See Figure 12)

The further we continue in our growth as the saints of God, the greater we increase our reward of glory.

*2 Corinthians 3:18 But we all, with open face beholding as in a glass the glory of the Lord, **are changed into the same image from glory to glory**, even as by the Spirit of the Lord.*

It's not until we get the blood, fire, and water in our lives are we eligible to move into a place of growth deserving of moon glory. When we find ourselves in the wilderness of testing and trials, we can rest

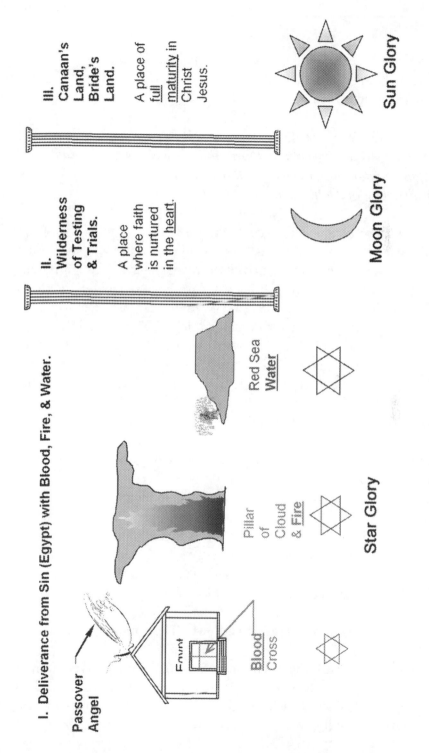

I. Deliverance from Sin (Egypt) with Blood, Fire, & Water.

Passover
Angel

Egypt

Blood
Cross

Star Glory

Pillar
of
Cloud
& Fire

Red Sea
Water

II.
Wilderness
of Testing
& Trials.

A place
where faith
is nurtured
in the heart.

Moon Glory

III.
Canaan's
Land,
Bride's
Land.

A place of
full
maturity in
Christ
Jesus.

Sun Glory

Figure 12.   Israel's & A Christian's Journey with Rewards.

135

assured that the moon glory is our reward. To grow up into the head of all things and walk in spiritual Canaan's land, we are walking with the glory of the Sun (See Figure 12).

*Philippians 3:13* *Brethren, I count not myself to have apprehended: but this one thing I do, forgetting those things which are behind, and reaching forth unto those things which are before, 14 I press toward the mark for the prize of the high calling of God in Christ Jesus.*

God wants us to reach for the highest goal, the mark for the prize of the high calling of God which is the Sun Glory. Similarly, the Mosaic Tabernacle shows the pattern of growth corresponding with the different degrees of reward (See Figure 13). As we learn how to apply more blood fire and water on our lives as the priests did in the Mosaic Tabernacle, we increase in our glory to a higher state of star glory. (See Figure 13)

Entering into the Holy Place is where we begin to learn to begin to pray as we find ourselves in trials and temptations. We learn to walk by the light of the Candle Stick, which is the word of God, and stop by the altar of prayer again on our way to the Table of Shewbread. This is where we can eat of the unleavened bread of Life to strengthen us that we may govern ourselves accordingly. From the Table of Shewbread, we must return to the altar of prayer before we crawl under the veil. At the Holy place, we can obtain the moon glory.

Under the veil and into the Holy of Holies is the only way into the glory of the sun, a place where we stand in the presence of God face to face with God. This is the place of full maturity. A bride must be fully mature before she can enter into a covenant with a bridegroom. Can you imagine the sun trying to place his arms around a star and loosing it in his own glory? The bride must have the glory of the Son to be His wife.

### The Higher One Goes In God, The Fewer The Numbers Will Be.

The bible records of the great multitude that was delivered from Egypt, only four people who originated from Egypt, entered into Canaan's Land; Joshua, Caleb, Gershom (Moses' son) and Eleazar (Aaron's son). And so it is with spiritual growth, the higher one grows,

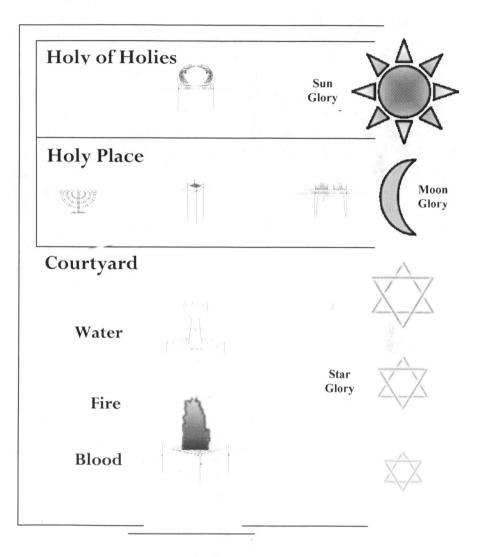

Figure 13. The Mosaic Tabernacle & Degrees of Reward

the fewer there are around him. Christians who do very little to further their relationship with God will always have someone around to entertain them. The Christians who pursue Jesus will find themselves separated from the multitudes that no man can number. The more we grow with God, the greater our reward in eternity. However, the spiritually mature ones also enjoy the favor of God on earth. By definition, favor isn't fair, it's just favor. As I mature in the Lord, I find that it is a pleasure to grow in Him and not drudgery. There are many benefits here on earth that are realized by those who receive favor of the Lord. Abram was obedient when God told him to come out from among his people. So Abram found favor with the Lord.

God is calling us to come out from among the people who keep us from serving Him to our fullest potential. To be a Christian is to be a separated people before God. This is our true way of Life!

*2 Corinthians 6:17  Wherefore come out from among them, and be ye separate, saith the Lord, and touch not the unclean thing; and I will receive you,*

**New Heaven (A Multitude No Man Can Number)**

The New Heaven is a place of a multitude that no man can number. God used the stars of the heavens when he promised Abram that he would be the father of a great nation to illustrate how great this people would be.

*Genesis 15: 3 And Abram said, Behold, to me thou hast given no seed: and, lo, one born in my house is mine heir.  4 And, behold, the word of the LORD came unto him, saying, This shall not be thine heir; but he that shall come forth out of thine own bowels shall be thine heir.  5 And he brought him forth abroad, and said, Look now toward heaven, and tell the stars, if thou be able to number them: and he said unto him, So shall thy seed be.*

When Israel started on the first third of their journey, they were a great and mixed multitude.

*Exodus 12: 37 ¶ And the children of Israel journeyed from Rameses to*

*Succoth, about six hundred thousand on foot that were men, beside children. 38 And a mixed multitude went up also with them; and flocks, and herds, even very much cattle.*

This number didn't include the women or children. When Israel gathered to offer their sacrifices in the Mosaic Tabernacle, all the people who had an offering would come into the courtyard while the priests performed their duties.

## New Earth (Four and Twenty Elders)

The New Earth is a place for kings and priests. The number that will receive this kind of glory will be considerably smaller than the New Heavens.

***Revelation 4:10** The four and twenty elders fall down before him that sat on the throne, and worship him that liveth for ever and ever, and cast their crowns before the throne, saying,*

In the second-third of rewards, they sat round about the throne, depicting a closer proximity to the throne of God. Our spiritual maturity will dictate how close we will be to the throne of God.

When Israel entered into the wilderness, the ground swallowed up many people for making a golden calf while Moses was in Mt. Sinai. There were several times that the sin of the congregation of Israel caused God's wrath to destroy some of them. Hence, the numbers were greatly reduced in the forty years of wandering in the wilderness. When we find ourselves confronted by the truth about our hearts, many turn back in discouragement. The multitude is reduced at every stage by the choices of the individuals not God.

In the Mosaic Tabernacle, the Holy Place was only visited by the priests and high priests. Hence the numbers were reduced tremendously at this stage.

## Sun Glory (One Bride)

In the New City, the glory required to live there will be the sun glory.

Here is where the street is made of gold. Most importantly, Jesus will be there and those who are in the New City will see Jesus face to face. This is where the pinnacle of life awaits our arrival. Let's take a look at a picture of the bride in her full glory.

*Revelation 12:1* ¶ *And there appeared a great wonder in heaven; a woman clothed with the sun, and the moon under her feet, and upon her head a crown of twelve stars:*

Isn't this a glorious picture of the Bride? When a child grows, they don't cut off an arm to obtain a larger arm. Likewise, when we gain a higher glory, we don't do away with the glory we already have, we simply add to what was already there.

In the Holy of Holies, the number reduces from the priests and the high priest to only the high priest. This is not to say that only one person can make it to the Sun Glory, rather to say that we must not be hesitant in choosing Jesus when confronted with the choice of keeping our friends or drawing closer to Him. You see, not everyone is willing to choose Jesus over all.

The number that makes it into the sun glory is shown in Revelations as 144,000. Whether this number is literal or figurative, I don't know. I do know that God wants all of us to grow into the full maturity of Jesus Christ and receive the sun glory. However, that is up to each of us.

*Revelation 14:1* ¶ *And I looked, and, lo, a Lamb stood on the mount Sion,* *and with him an hundred forty [and] four thousand, having his Father's name written in their foreheads. 2   And I heard a voice from heaven, as the voice of many waters, and as the voice of a great thunder: and I heard the voice of harpers harping with their harps: 3   And they sung as it were a new song before the throne, and before the four beasts, and the elders: and no man could learn that song but the hundred and forty and four thousand, which were redeemed from the earth. 4   These are they which were not defiled with women; for they are virgins. These are they which follow the Lamb whithersoever he goeth. These were redeemed from among men, being the firstfruits unto God and to the Lamb. 5   And in their mouth was found no guile: for they are without fault before the throne of God.*

Let us be determined to forget those things which are behind us and press on toward the mark of the High calling; Canaan's Land, The Holy of Holies, The Sun Glory, The New City, The Bride of Christ!

# 7

---

---

# GARMENT REWARDS
## FOR
## GROWTH

### *(White Robes, White Raiment & Fine Linen)*

In a kingdom, garments signify one's rank or position in the kingdom. The higher one goes in a kingdom, the more garments he will wear.

*Hebrews 11:6 But without faith [it is] impossible to please [him]: for he that cometh to God must believe that he is, and [that] he is a rewarder of them that diligently seek him.*

God does reward those who diligently seek Him, not only on earth but in heaven as well. To reiterate, the reward received is proportionate to the growth achieved here on earth. We must not only grow but watch and keep our growth. Note in Hebrews 16:15 that we are to be diligent to keep our garments that we have obtained.

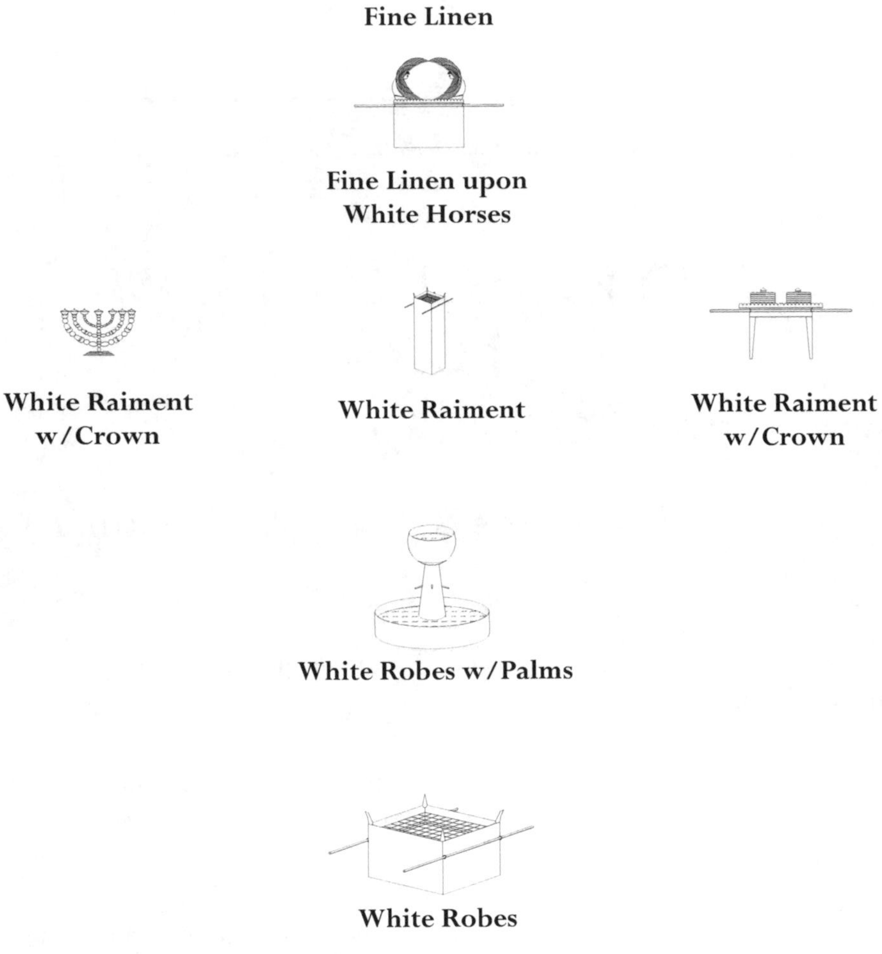

**Fine Linen**

**Fine Linen upon
White Horses**

**White Raiment
w/Crown**

**White Raiment**

**White Raiment
w/Crown**

**White Robes w/Palms**

**White Robes**

**Figure 14. The Mosaic Tabernacle & Garments of Reward.**

***Revelations 16:15*** *Behold, I come as a thief. Blessed is he that watcheth, and keepeth his **garments**, lest he walk naked, and they see his shame.*

Just as a farmer or gardener keeps their fields or garden, there is much that must be done to keep the garden of our hearts free from weeds, insects and rodents that can destroy the fruit of our labor. In the context of this chapter, let us ensure that our garments are in good condition, free from the moths of sin and rot of poor character.

Among the many garments mentioned in the word of God, there are only three that are clearly depicted as a reward; white robes, white raiment and fine linen. Let's take a look at these garments.

**White Robes.**

***Revelation 6:9*** ¶ *And when he had opened the fifth seal, I saw under the altar the souls of them that were slain for the word of God, and for the testimony which they held:* **10** *And they cried with a loud voice, saying, How long, O Lord, holy and true, dost thou not judge and avenge our blood on them that dwell on the earth?* **11** *And **white robes** were given unto every one of them; and it was said unto them, that they should rest yet for a little season, until their fellowservants also and their brethren, that should be killed as they [were], should be fulfilled.*

The Greek word for white robes is στολη stole (stol-ay') which describes a long loose outer garment that extends to the feet and is worn by kings, priests and persons of rank. Its root word στελλω stello (stel' –lo) extends the meaning to include set in order, to be equipped and prepared. From the very beginning of our walk with Christ we are equipped to begin our journey as kings and priests.

**Their Disposition**

When Jesus, said "father forgive them for they know not what they do", we can deduct that these souls had not reached this level of maturity because they were asking the Lord for revenge. The altar they were under was the Brazin Altar.

It's common for immature Christians who are suffering for Christ's sake to want to see God's wrath upon their offenders. A mature Christian knows that it is a dangerous thing to fall into the hands of an angry God and would not wish that on those who are walking in darkness, with hopes that they will come into His marvelous light. Many are persecuted unto death for Christ and the defining reward is their disposition at the time of death. Stephen is another picture of maturity.

*Acts 7:59   And they stoned Stephen, calling upon [God], and saying, Lord Jesus, receive my spirit. 60   And he kneeled down, and cried with a loud voice, **Lord, lay not this sin to their charge**. And when he had said this, he fell asleep.*

Stephen was truly mature to care for His offenders greater than His own life. Isn't that just like Jesus?

Revelations 6:9-11 clearly shows that our disposition and attitudes will follow us in heaven and in fact, determine our reward at the judgment seat. Going to heaven will not solve our bad attitude and immaturity. Though we will continue our development after our reward has been received, we should not allow ourselves to stagnate in our development here on earth.

**White Robes with Palms in their hands.**

In addition to the garments one would wear in a kingdom to reflect nobility, what one carried in his hands distinguished his level of authority as well.

*Revelation 7:9 After this I beheld, and, lo, a great multitude, which no man could number, of all nations, and kindreds, and people, and tongues, stood before the throne, and before the Lamb, **clothed with white robes, and palms in their hands**; 10 And cried with a loud voice, saying, Salvation to our God which sitteth upon the throne, and unto the Lamb.*

Palms speak of higher authority and position. In Matthew 21:8, the people spread clothes and branches before the Lord as he entered Israel. What an

incredible tool for worship for someone to take their authority and position and lay it down at the feet of Jesus (See Figure 14).
**White Raiment**

*Revelation 3:4 Thou hast a few names even in Sardis which have not defiled their garments; and they shall walk with me in white: for they are worthy. 5 He that overcometh, the same shall be clothed in **white raiment**; and I will not blot out his name out of the book of life, but I will confess his name before my Father, and before his angels.*

The Greek word for white raiment is ιματιον himation (him-at' -ee-on) described as a cloak or mantle and the tunic worn as an upper garment. In the kingdom of God, those who wear white raiment over their white robes are walking in a higher maturity and position with the Lord.

*Revelation 3:18 I counsel thee to buy of me gold tried in the fire, that thou mayest be rich; and **white raiment**, that thou mayest be clothed, and [that] the shame of thy nakedness do not appear; and anoint thine eyes with eyesalve, that thou mayest see.*

Chapter 7 places the seven churches at each of the seven pieces of furniture in the tabernacle. The location of the church of Sardis is in the Holy Place which will further support that white raiment is awarded to those who have achieved the growth of the Holy Place (See Figure 15).

**White Raiment with Crowns of Gold**

*Revelation 4:4 And round about the throne [were] four and twenty seats: and upon the seats I saw four and twenty elders sitting, **clothed in white raiment; and they had on their heads crowns of gold.***

To wear a crown in addition to the white raiment is to point out yet a higher level in the Holy Place that can be reached. The Greek word for crown is στεφανοj stephanos (stef' -an-os) and has a primary root *stepho* which is defined as to twine or a wreathe. Stefanos is a mark of royalty or exalted rank which is the reward of righteousness one can obtain.

*Re 16:15 Behold, I come as a thief. Blessed is he that **watcheth, and keepeth his garments**, lest he walk naked, and they see his shame.*

Keeping one's garments requires consistent feeding in the word of God, prayer and work in the ministry. Just as a plant is incapable of existing in a stable state, it is either growing or dying, so is our spiritual life. At this level of growth and reward, keeping the garments intact is a pleasure and not laborious. Always remember that complacency is a sure way to lose your progress in the Lord.

**Fine Linen**

*Re 19:8 And to her was granted that she should be arrayed in **fine linen**, clean and white: for the fine linen is the righteousness of saints.*

Fine linen is depicted as βυσσοj bussos (boos' –sos) which is linen made from byssus, which is very costly, delicate, soft and white. This material is refined by being pierced with a needle many times to soften its texture. This is the bride of Christ's clothing. She has been pierced just as her bridegroom to refine her that she would learn obedience thru the things she suffered. In order for the fine linen to be clean or καψαροj katharos (kath-ar-os'), it had to be purified by fire, free from corrupt desire, sin and guilt as well as unstained with the guilt of anything.

*Revelation 19:7 Let us be glad and rejoice, and give honour to him: for the marriage of the Lamb is come, **and his wife hath made herself ready.** 8 And to her was granted that she should be arrayed in fine linen, clean and white: for the fine linen is the righteousness of saints.*

Remember that the subject of growing to the measure and stature of Jesus Christ is not about salvation. This is about making ourselves ready for our bride groom. The bride doesn't prepare herself for the wedding to start a relationship; she prepares herself willingly because of the relationship. Her motive is surrounded by the excitement of her relationship coming to a milestone in her journey. So we should be motivated by the excitement of our relationship with our groom; Jesus.

The bride of Christ will distinguish herself above the wedding party by making herself ready. The best way we can make ourselves ready is to pursue maturity in the Lord.

**Fine Linen Upon White Horses**

*Re 19:14 And the armies which were in heaven followed him **upon white horses, clothed in fine linen, white and clean.***

You can see that those with fine linen and riding a white horse is a different level than those who were only given fine linen and clearly demonstrates that there are different degrees at this stage of maturity as well. It is one thing to be a bride, a higher level to be a wife and the highest level to bring forth a child as a mother (See Figure 14).

These armies went to war against the beast and the false prophet who were then cast into the lake of fire. They went to war beside the Lord. What a great honor it will be for the bride to stand beside her bridegroom to destroy the enemies of God! Not only will she be arrayed in fine linen, clean and white, but her authority and mentality will follow Philippians 2:5-9.

*Philippians 2:5 Let this mind be in you, which was also in Christ Jesus: 6 Who, being in the form of God, thought it not robbery to be equal with God: 7 But made himself of no reputation, and took upon him the form of a servant, and was made in the likeness of men: 8 And being found in fashion as a man, he humbled himself, and became obedient unto death, even the death of the cross. 9 Wherefore God also hath highly exalted him, and given him a name which is above every name:*

# 8

## THE SEVEN CHURCHES

In today's world, there are many different denominations and churches. Regardless of the church name or denomination, all churches that name Jesus as the son of God, fall into one of seven categories depicted by the seven churches of Asia Minor mentioned in Revelations chapters 1-3 (See Figure 15). They represent different levels of spiritual maturity. When placing each church on the tabernacle, it is best to follow the same order as the High Priest's followed as they moved towards the Holy of Holies, thus we can see each church's level of maturity. Each one of today's churches can be placed in one of the seven categories by its revelation of the word, the tribulations they're currently facing and the walk by which the pastor of that church lives and teaches. The congregation plays a small part in the maturity of the church as a whole because the pastor will bring the congregation to his level of revelation in time. This is a clear support why all the churches are necessary at the level of maturity they represent because they all create one body of our Lord Jesus Christ. Without the foot, how would the body stand? The first two churches are readily located on the tabernacle by their doctrinal beliefs. The rest are better positioned by their teachings of the inward man, his disposition, attitudes and the ability of the people to apply the word of God in their daily lives.

Each of the seven churches plays an important role in the body Christ. This is why the enemy would have the denominations and churches fighting against one another. One of the enemy's tricks is to convince a congregation or denomination that all the other Jesus believing churches fall short of God. This spirit of pride destroys the power of unity available to the body of Christ. Also, we must realize that all born-again believers are part of the body of Christ. Let's not confuse the anointing and revelation we receive at our church because we are faithful there with a separating spirit that tries to convince us that our church is the only one. For we know that *__all__* who seek will find, *__all__* who knock it will be opened and *__all__* who ask shall receive.

As we move from one stage to the next in our study of the seven churches, we will find specific tribulations which we must endure and gain the victory as we grow in God. The tribulations alone do not pin point a position of a saint or church. We must include many factors to discern the spiritual maturity of a saint or a church. To reach the top as a saint, we must seek a place of worship where the Lord has anointed us to be fed and grow.

There are times when we are called out of a church to move to the next level. It's not that the church can't grow; it's just that the church may not move at a specific pace God has set for an individual. However, God does not use confusion to spur an individual on to another church, unlike the enemy. Jesus causes others to move on peacefully. Anything else would dictate that God is pruning the individual and he should allow the Lord to finish the work before considering a move. We must remember that God corrects those whom He loves. Sometimes this form of correction comes in the way of difficulties in the church. Let's not forget:

*Proverbs 27:17; "Iron sharpeneth iron; so a man sharpeneth the countenance of his friend."*

To be sharpened, there must be friction.

As we cover the seven churches, refer to Figure 15 often to see the position the church has been placed in the tabernacle. Also if you refer to Figures 13 and 14, you can see the glory and garments assigned to each church according to their position.

| HOLY OF HOLIES | | |
| --- | --- | --- |
| | Leodicea | |
| |  | |
| | Philadelphia | |

| HOLY PLACE | | |
| --- | --- | --- |
| Thyatira | Pergamos | Sardis |

COURTYARD

Smyrna

Ephesus

**Figure 15. The Mosaic Tabernacle & the Seven Churches.**

**EPHESUS (The Blood)**

*Revelation 2:1 ¶ Unto the angel of the church of Ephesus write; These things saith he that holdeth the seven stars in his right hand, who walketh in the midst of the seven golden candlesticks; 2 I know thy works, and thy labour, and thy patience, and how thou canst not bear them which are evil: and thou hast tried them which say they are apostles, and are not, and hast found them liars: 3 And hast borne, and hast patience, and for my name's sake hast laboured, and hast not fainted. 4 Nevertheless I have [somewhat] against thee, because thou hast left thy first love. 5 Remember therefore from whence thou art fallen, and repent, and do the first works; or else I will come unto thee quickly, and will remove thy candlestick out of his place, except thou repent. 6 But this thou hast, that thou hatest the deeds of the Nicolaitans, which I also hate. 7 He that hath an ear, let him hear what the Spirit saith unto the churches; To him that overcometh will I give to eat of the tree of life, which is in the midst of the paradise of God.*

The root word for Ephesus is **Εφεσος** Ephesos (*ef'-es-os*). Interestingly enough, its name means to be permitted. After the blood is applied at the altar, Ephesus is permitted to move higher in the things of God. When reading this scripture, I can't help but notice how powerful and capable the Ephesians were.

All churches that have the revelation that the Lord Jesus Christ is the son of God, that He was born of a virgin, died on the cross for our sins, rose again the third day and is sitting at the right hand of the father falls at least into the Ephesus category. It's not uncommon to see churches whose doctrine prescribes only to the blood of Christ as diligent and fervent about their father's business in the house of God. Just as a new babe in Christ is willing to do anything for the Lord in gratitude for the burden lifting experience, so is the Ephesus church in their first love.

**EPHESUS (The Blood & Fire)**

The churches that have the revelation of the blood of Christ and the Baptism of the Holy Ghost with the evidence of speaking in unknown tongues is a higher level of spiritual maturity at the Brazin Altar. This church realizes the importance of being lead and guided by the Holy

Ghost. They teach that the fire is vital to spiritual growth and cannot be circumvented when one is seeking a more mature relationship. Speaking in tongues is an effective countermeasure to leaving our first love (See Figure 15).

### Temptation of Leaving Our First Love:

Leaving our first love with Christ is undoubtedly a dangerous situation. If we are to mature into the bride of Christ, then we must never leave our first love and first works. Many saints and churches start out on fire for God and end up as smoldering coal. Repenting and returning to our first works is the only way to rekindle our fire of first love.

A while back, I bought a piece of land that required some clearing. As we began to clear the land, we started a fire to burn the brush. The fire grew until its flames reached twenty feet at times. The next day when the fire had burned to ashes, only a small stream of smoke rose from the pile of ashes. As I approached it I couldn't feel the radiating heat that I felt the day before. The fire had died down due to lack of fuel. I went to the ashes and began stirring the coals. The coals began to glow again, I could feel the radiant heat begin to increase and I was able to burn again without lighting another fire. This is likened to when we stop feeding our fire for Christ; we can reduce to a smoldering pile of ashes. However, we have the power to stir up the gift that is within us to bring our fire back to a roar with the fuel of the word and prayer. Getting around others that are on fire aid in the speed of recovery, likewise, continuing with those who are dead or smoldering in their walk with Him will speed up a decrease in our fire.

### SMYRNA (The Blood, Fire and Water)

*Revelation 2:8 ¶ And unto the angel of the church in Smyrna write; These things saith the first and the last, which was dead, and is alive; 9 I know thy works, and tribulation, and poverty, (but thou art rich) and [I know] the blasphemy of them which say they are Jews, and are not, but [are] the synagogue of Satan. 10 Fear none of those things which thou shalt suffer: behold, the devil shall cast [some] of you into prison that ye may be tried; and ye shall have tribulation ten days: be thou faithful unto death, and I will give thee a crown of life. 11 He that hath an ear, let him hear what the Spirit saith unto the churches; He that overcometh shall not be hurt of the second death.*

The root word for Smyrna is **σμυρνα** Smurna *(smoor'-nah)* which translates to myrrh. Not only was myrrh used as a perfume, it was used for embalming as well. What a beautiful picture of standing before the mirror of the word (the Brazin Altar) and crucifying the flesh seen in the reflection of the word with the blood, fire and washing of the water of the word. This very act is a sweet smelling savor or perfume to the Lord. As we embalm our old man, the Lord describes it as a sweet smelling savor.

Smyrna is located at the Brazin Laver where the water is used for baptism once, and then to wash the feet and hands of the priests daily. Along with the water, this brass or looking glass was as a mirror for them to be reminded who they were and also for them to try those who were imposters in the Jewish family. Self examination or judgment was done here by comparing themselves to the mirror of the word of God.

Churches that have the revelation of baptism as a necessary requirement for spiritual growth and the daily washing of the water (Word of God) to renew the mind fall into this category. Self examination, reconciliation, and reprioritizing as the Lord leads are taught as a way of life here. Churches that admonish the body to be baptized in Jesus' name are preparing them for the next step as one who desires to be the bride of Christ.

**Temptation:**

Fear of persecution is a real issue for many. None of us like to face rejection. The world trains us to be concerned of what others think or say. We are taught that what others think of us defines our self-worth and that to fit in, blend in with the crowd, or to be cool you must do what "everyone else is doing". Have you ever noticed that the world's definition of "everyone else" usually excludes those who are living the life of Christ? This kind of peer pressure contributes to the fears we deal with concerning persecution from the people we've allowed to dictate to us our value. We must continually stay in the word of God to allow the reflection of who God has made us and where our self-worth truly comes from to remind us that we are more than conquerors.

## PERGAMOS (All of the above plus Prayer, Intercession and Travail)

*Revelation 2:12 ¶ And to the angel of the church in Pergamos write; These things saith he which hath the sharp sword with two edges; 13 I know thy works, and where thou dwellest, [even] where Satan's seat [is]: and thou holdest fast my name, and hast not denied my faith, even in those days wherein Antipas [was] my faithful martyr, who was slain among you, where Satan dwelleth. 14 But I have a few things against thee, because thou hast there them that hold the doctrine of Balaam, who taught Balac to cast a stumblingblock before the children of Israel, to eat things sacrificed unto idols, and to commit fornication. 15 So hast thou also them that hold the doctrine of the Nicolaitans, which thing I hate. 16 Repent; or else I will come unto thee quickly, and will fight against them with the sword of my mouth. 17 He that hath an ear, let him hear what the Spirit saith unto the churches; To him that overcometh will I give to eat of the hidden manna, and will give him a white stone, and in the stone a new name written, which no man knoweth saving he that receiveth [it].*

Pergamos comes from the Greek word περγαμος Pergamos (*per'-gam-os)* and is interpreted as "height or elevation". With the church of Pergamos placed at the Golden Altar of Incense, is it any surprise that our height and elevation in the spirit is directly linked to our prayer life? A majority of things revealed by God take place at the time of prayer. Those who capitalize on this point will find themselves in a position of heightened status.

### Temptation

With increased growth there are benefits that come with such a position. The temptation is to allow these remunerations rather than the Lord to dictate our decision making process. Balak, King of Moab wanted to bribe the Lord's prophet to curse the Israelites. Balaam knew that the Israelites were God's people and yet he violated the principle of touching God's anointed. For his actions, God was prepared to destroy Balaam. We must remember that every saved person, regardless of their developed maturity level, is anointed of God. When we backbite, persecute, plot against, or compete with, we are touching His anointed. This principle will work for us when we work with it and against us if we violate it.

Committing fornication takes place in the heart first. The temptation of lust is destructive to our prayer life. We must continually plead the Blood, moment by moment if necessary, to stay clean before the Lord that we may approach the next step.

Churches that teach the congregation to study their heart in prayer will be found at the Golden Altar of Incense where the heart of the tabernacle resides. In studying their heart, they must be aware that they cannot trust their own heart above the word of God and the Lord Jesus Christ.

*Jeremiah 17:9    The heart [is] deceitful above all [things], and desperately wicked: who can know it?*

The answer to this question is simple; Jesus knows the depths of our heart. Along with showing us the things of our lives that line up with His word, He will expose our hidden agendas, our motives, our attempts to manipulate, and our perverse ways.

There is a place in our spiritual walk that requires us to be aware of these issues and to navigate through this spiritual landmine with effectual fervent prayer. Regardless of our successes or failures, we must not marvel at what God has done through us to the point that we forget that yesterday's sacrifice is insufficient for today. What have you done for the Lord today?

**THYATIRA (All of the above plus Walking by the Word)**

*Revelation 2:18 ¶ And unto the angel of the church in Thyatira write; These things saith the Son of God, who hath his eyes like unto a flame of fire, and his feet [are] like fine brass; 19 I know thy works, and charity, and service, and faith, and thy patience, and thy works; and the last [to be] more than the first. 20 Notwithstanding I have a few things against thee, because thou sufferest that woman Jezebel, which calleth herself a prophetess, to teach and to seduce my servants to commit fornication, and to eat things sacrificed unto idols. 21 And I gave her space to repent of her fornication; and she repented not. 22 Behold, I will cast her into a bed, and them that commit adultery with her into great tribulation, except they repent of their deeds. 23 And I will kill her children with death; and all the churches shall know that I am he which searcheth the reins and hearts: and I will give unto every one of you according to your works. 24 But unto you I say, and unto the rest in Thyatira, as many as have not this doctrine, and which have not known the depths of Satan, as they speak; I will put upon you none other burden. 25 But that which ye have [already] hold fast till I come. 26 And he that overcometh, and keepeth my works unto the end, to him will I give power over the nations: 27 And he shall rule them with a rod of iron; as the vessels of a potter shall they be broken to shivers: even as I received of my Father. 28 And I will give him the morning star. 29 He that hath an ear, let him hear what the Spirit saith unto the churches.*

The Greek word for Thyatira is θυατειρα Thuateira (*thoo-at'-i-rah*) which means "odor of affliction". Placed at the Golden Candlestick which was a beaten work, it stands to reason that the church at this maturity level understands the importance of learning obedience through the things which are suffered. We may be appalled by the odor of affliction but God finds it appealing. He knows that we achieve a greater degree of obedience when we suffer affliction for His sake. When we aspire to walk by the word of God, regardless of cost, we will experience this affliction in due course.

Churches that have the revelation of the blessed necessity to walk by the word of God and suffer for Christ's sake while receiving revelations of the word of God will find themselves at the Golden Candlestick. The greater the suffering or humility we experience, the greater the revelation of the word of God we will receive. Receiving revelations from the word of God is an honor, if we are willing to pay the price; there is no limit to the depths of His word. Hence Proverbs 15:33 says;

**Proverbs 15:33** ¶ *The fear of the LORD [is] the instruction of wisdom; and before honour [is] humility.*

**Temptation**

When a leader abuses his authority under the auspices of causing others to suffer for Christ sake, a perversion of the principle of suffering for Christ sake begins to develop. Jezebel usurped the authority of God, her king and her husband. She disrespected authority while demanding others to respect her. The Jezebel spirit is a hard task master, causing many to commit spiritual fornication and adultery. When we start seeing some spiritual progress in our lives, we must ensure that we don't exalt ourselves above measure.

Committing spiritual fornication takes place when a Christian esteems something or someone greater than the Lord Jesus Christ. As their maturity develops into the bride of Christ, this same sin falls under spiritual adultery. Let us not worship anything other than the Lord Jesus Christ.

**SARDIS (All of the above plus Strength from the Word)**

***Revelation 3:1*** ¶ *And unto the angel of the church in Sardis write; These things saith he that hath the seven Spirits of God, and the seven stars; I know thy works, that thou hast a name that thou livest, and art dead. 2 Be watchful, and strengthen the things which remain, that are ready to die: for I have not found thy works perfect before God. 3 Remember therefore how thou hast received and heard, and hold fast, and repent. If therefore thou shalt not watch, I will come on thee as a thief, and thou shalt not know what hour I will come upon thee. 4 Thou hast a few names even in Sardis which have not defiled their garments; and they shall walk with me in white: for they are worthy. 5 He that overcometh, the same shall be clothed in white raiment; and I will not blot out his name out of the book of life, but I will confess his name before my Father, and before his angels. 6 He that hath an ear, let him hear what the Spirit saith unto the churches.*

Sardis in Greek is σαρδεις Sardis *(sar'-dice)* which translates to "red ones". What a tremendous picture of one who continually stays under the blood for not only forgiveness, but for sanctification, purification and strength. Sardis is located at the Golden Table of

Shewbread where they were to be watchful and strengthen the things that remain in their lives by the bread of the word.

Churches that have the revelation of watching and trusting in God's word to give us strength when we are weak can be found at the Golden Table of Shewbread. Here, the Christian learns to run to the word for strength and encouragement rather than people, places and things. Verse 2 clearly states the mission of this place of maturity; we must be watchful and strengthen the things which remain. These things that remain are the things that have passed through the fire and stand the testing and trials from the Altar of Incense of Prayer and the Word from the Golden Candlestick. As the Lord develops us, we will be required to be willing to offer our all to the sacrifice. Those things that remain from His purging, we must strengthen by the word of God.

**Temptation:**

The temptation to be complacent here is great. Many of the things we have received with such reverence are sometimes treated as common experience. We can fall to the dangers of desensitization of living in the presence of the Lord and forget to watch and pray. When we are so presumptuous as to approach the Lord with such familiarity, we stand at the threshold of contempt. Let us watch, pray and repent for our presumptuous sin.

## LAODICEA (All of the Above plus Full maturity without Humility)

_Revelation 3:14 ¶ And unto the angel of the church of the Laodiceans write; These things saith the Amen, the faithful and true witness, the beginning of the creation of God; 15 I know thy works, that thou art neither cold nor hot: I would thou wert cold or hot. 16 So then because thou art lukewarm, and neither cold nor hot, I will spue thee out of my mouth. 17 Because thou sayest, I am rich, and increased with goods, and have need of nothing; and knowest not that thou art wretched, and miserable, and poor, and blind, and naked: 18 I counsel thee to buy of me gold tried in the fire, that thou mayest be rich; and white raiment, that thou mayest be clothed, and [that] the shame of thy nakedness do not appear; and anoint thine eyes with eyesalve, that thou mayest see. 19 As_ *many as I love, I rebuke and chasten: be zealous therefore, and repent. 20 Behold, I stand at the door, and knock: if any man hear my voice, and open the door, I will come in to him, and will sup with him, and he with me. 21 To him that overcometh will I grant to sit with me in my throne, even as I also overcame, and am set down with my Father in his throne. 22 He that hath an ear, let him hear what the Spirit saith unto the churches.*

The Greek translation for Laodiceans comes from the root word λαοδικευς Laodikeia (*lah-od-ik'-i-ah*) which means "justice of the people". The place of the Mercy Seat is the appropriate place of the Laodiceans when it comes to justice for the people of God. In its purest sense, the mind of God was presented at this level of maturity between the cherubim. Among many things, the mind of God passes judgment on deeds, words, actions, motives and all hidden agendas. Those who obtain this level of maturity go through extensive scrutiny from God before they are able to receive and relay His mind to others. Much wisdom, knowledge, and revelation resides in this position.

The church that falls into this category has many gifts, talents, and a strong revelation of the word of God, knowledge of the Word and Spirit is at its peak. All that is needed to make it into the bride is obtained and the work of the ministry has been brought to new dimensions in the body of Christ.

**Temptation:**

At this level of maturity the temptation of thinking that one has arrived, or finished the race, is strong. Just because the Lord has taught us all that we know doesn't mean that He has taught us all that He knows. The deception of having obtained all that can be obtained in the Lord is fueled by self admiration of what the Lord has done through them. Spiritual pride is a predominant problem at this level. The lack of submission to the word and authority begins to creep into many lives here. Is it any wonder that Lucifer fell by this same self admiration? Once we have been convinced that we are rich and have need of nothing, we will become lukewarm in our actions and service to our Lord.

We can remedy this challenge by submitting ourselves, humbling our wills to be subjected to the word of God all over again. By taking all that we've learned, obtained, and earned in the natural and spiritual realm and placing it at the feet of Jesus to do with as He wills, we find ourselves with the liberty to love Him in awe again.

## PHILADELPHIA (All of the above plus Full maturity tempered with Humility)

**_Revelation 3:7_** ¶ _And to the angel of the church in Philadelphia write; These things saith he that is holy, he that is true, he that hath the key of David, he that openeth, and no man shutteth; and shutteth, and no man openeth; 8 I know thy works: behold, I have set before thee an open door, and no man can shut it: for thou hast a little strength, and hast kept my word, and hast not denied my name. 9 Behold, I will make them of the synagogue of Satan, which say they are Jews, and are not, but do lie; behold, I will make them to come and worship before thy feet, and to know that I have loved thee. 10 Because thou hast kept the word of my patience, I also will keep thee from the hour of temptation, which shall come upon all the world, to try them that dwell upon the earth. 11 Behold, I come quickly: hold that fast which thou hast, that no man take thy crown. 12 Him that overcometh will I make a pillar in the temple of my God, and he shall go no more out: and I will write upon him the name of my God, and the name of the city of my God, [which is] new Jerusalem, which cometh down out of heaven from my God: and [I will write upon him] my new name. 13 He that hath an ear, let him hear what the Spirit saith unto the churches._

In order to place anything into the Ark of the Covenant, it would have to pass through the Mercy Seat first. Therefore, the greatest church mentioned in Asia Minor is the church of Philadelphia. This is the highest level of maturity, the Ark of the Covenant; a place where all that is known in all the other levels of maturity has been obtained coupled with the purposeful choice to submit underneath the judgment and leading of the Lord; the disposition of counting all things but dung compared to the Lord Jesus Christ. I would like to point out that this is the only church that the Lord did not mention a flaw. Could it be that the Lord saw perfect humility? Humility with little knowledge is great, but humility with great knowledge is best.

Also, God built the tabernacle from His lofty position down to the lowly position of man. The Ark of the Covenant was the first piece of furniture built. Although it seems that the last church mentioned would be the greatest, the Mercy Seat (the Laodiceans) was supported by the Ark. The Mercy Seat would not be in His proper place without resting above and upon the Ark.

The Greek translation of Philadelphia is φιλαδελφεια Philadelphia (*fil-ad-el'-fee-ah*) which means "brotherly love". Jesus said in John 15:13:

**John 15:13** *Greater love hath no man than this, that a man lay down his life for his friends.*

True love is the fulcrum of the balance between mercy and judgment. Many have obtained the ability to judge but have not tempered the sword of judgment with love. If they were asked to suffer the punishment that they have dealt to others, they would wince at the thought. Let us have a desire to balance mercy and judgment on others as well as ourselves.

While meditating one day, the Lord brought me out of my body and took me to an orbit around the earth. I saw a tether below me that connected me to my physical body. I was looking at the earth from space and I saw a hand with the strength to crush the earth hold it at the axis between the thumb and second finger. Without being told, I knew that this was the Lord's hand. The Lord pointed out to me that His strength wasn't in His ability to destroy the earth with just two fingers (which He could have done), but rather in His sensitivity and ability to apply just enough pressure that the earth could be held in place and still spin at the axis to maintain life. How much more should we as Christians strive to resist the temptation of letting someone have our entire wrath and apply only enough effort as is necessary to maintain life? Isn't that life more abundantly, to allow others to live without being destroyed by our insensitivity?

Truly the Church that has obtained this kind of Love in all that they do and say would be found at the Ark of the Covenant. The disposition here is one of servitude towards others in that they think of others before themselves. All of their gifts, talents, possessions, time, and money is towards the work of the Lord with the hope that some might be saved.

They concentrate on what is the LIFE decision rather than the right decision. Their mindset is as follows:

Not our will Lord, but thy will be done!
Forgive those who persecute us Lord for they know not what they do!
Let us surrender our Life to the Lord so that we might assist some towards salvation and maturity.

# 9

## *PRAYING THROUGH THE TABERNACLE*

Every time we kneel to pray, we in a sense begin the priest's journey through the tabernacle. Many of us stop short in our prayers and for this I would like to share how I walk through my tabernacle with the principles that I have given. Throughout this process, I journalize things that I receive of the Lord, and would like to encourage you to do the same.

Please know that I am not dictating your prayer life, rather giving you an outline of the process to move through the Tabernacle in your heart. The Holy Ghost will lead you and guide you into all truth, trust Him! My advice to those of you who need a step-by-step outline is to start with this and seek to be led by the Holy Ghost. To those of you who need to feel less regimented, try placing your liberty at each of these stations and see how the Holy Ghost leads you. All in all, have fun seeking Jesus! He is an exciting Lord who has wondrous things for all of us.

## The Brazin Altar

### Blood

Lord Forgive me of my sin's known and unknown. Cover me with your blood and help me live righteously before you.

### Fire
---Speak in Tongues ---

## The Brazin Laver

### Water – Cleansing of the Word
---Read the word to show where I'm right and wrong---
---Thank Him for bringing me to a place of maturity to do the things that I've gotten right---
---Repent for the wrong and ask the Lord to show me how to correct it, to better please Him---

## Golden Alter of Incense

### Prayer
--- The Lord's Prayer ---
---Ask the Lord for things spiritual and natural, to include the prayer of Jabez---
---Intercede for others and myself---
---Travail to bring the things of God into Birth---
---Pray for the Mercy of God on my enemies---

## Golden Candle Stick

### The Light of the Word
---Search the Word for a deeper revelation of Jesus---
---Learn at the feet of Jesus principles to walk by---
---Use the light of the word to show me where and how to go in and come out before Him---

**Golden Table of Shewbread**

**Bread – Strength of the Word**
---Seek strength to be obedient to His principles and the path he has
shown me to walk from the Word and prayer ---

**Mercy Seat**

**Mercy for Passage to the mind of Christ**
---Listen to hear His living voice strong in my heart---
---Obtain His Mercy that endures forever that I may pass it on to
others---

**Ark of Covenant**

**Sacrificial Love and Submission**
---Humble myself to submit in obedience to all that I have been
taught---
---Seek for the Life out of His Law---
---Love Others as Christ loves them---

# CONCLUSION

God set a pattern and repeated it to show the Christian the pathway to spiritual maturity. Israel's journey from Egypt to Canaan's Land typifies the Christian's journey to maturity. The Priest's journey from the Brazin Alter to the Holy of Holies shows the repeated process. In addition, the tabernacle displays the antidote to the challenges faced during Israel's journey. For example, when Israel was in the second portion of their journey, the wilderness, a place of testing and trials, God provided the Holy Place, the second portion of the tabernacle, a place of prayer, as the antidote or a way to get a solution for their trials.

The Tabernacle is also a perfect measuring stick to determine your growth. It's our family growth chart! By reading what I have presented, it is my prayer that you have been able to see where you are spiritually and understand the next step a little better. I hope that you saw more of Jesus and that you have grown closer to Him. I close with the sayings of Paul:

*Philippians 3:12 Not as though I had already attained, either were already perfect: but I follow after, if that I may apprehend that for which also I am apprehended of Christ Jesus. 13 Brethren, I count not myself to have apprehended: but [this] one thing [I do], forgetting those things which are behind, and reaching forth unto those things which are before,* **14 I press toward the mark for the prize of the high calling of God in Christ Jesus.**

In His Hands,

Pastor Steve

# *REFERENCES*

Hebrew and Chaldee Lexicon to the Old Testament, Gesenius and Fürst, Boston: A.I. Bradley & Co.

James Strong, Abingdon's Strong's Exhaustive Concordance of the Bible, New Jersey, 1890 – James Strong, Key Word Comparison 1980 – Abingdon

*Precious Gem in the Tabernacle,* Reverend B. R. Hicks, Indiana: Christ Gospel Press, 1961

Software: *Online Bible Edition*, Authorized Version of the King James Bible, Strong's Concordance
Version 2.00.04, June 2006

Thompson Chain Reference Study Bible King James Version, Kirkbride Bible Company, Inc. Indiana, 1988

The front cover photo came from www.christianphotos.net. The back photo came from archives of the Hubble Telescope.

**Pastor Steve Morgan** is an associate pastor at Son Light Covenant Church, Crestview, FL lead by Senior Pastor Alvin Smith. Pastor Morgan is the founder of FOR HIM Ministries, has traveled, and ministered in Europe as well as in the States as a prophet, pastor and evangelist. Originally, from Tampa, Florida, he has been serving the Lord since May 2, 1982. His calling was made known to him three months after he was saved. He entered a vow to keep his calling in his heart until the Lord showed it to his headship and his headship acknowledged it. While he waited, he occupied his time serving in many capacities in the church lifting up the vision of his headship and preparing himself in the word of God. Eighteen years later, June 1, 2000, he was fully ordained as a minister of the Gospel under Bishop Nathanial Holcomb of Covenant Connections International and Christian House of Prayer, Killeen, TX. Pastor Steve is also an Alumni of Sonship School of the First Born, Killen, TX.

As a United States Air Force Reservist, he was activated and sent to Pakistan and Jordan during the response of the Terrorist attacks on American soil on September 11, 2001. The bulk of this book was written on Pakistani and Jordanian soil. Pastor Steve's visit to Egypt in 2004 had an influence in encouraging him to publish this book.

Pastor Morgan is now visiting churches to share this message. He can be reached, at forhimmin@cox.net. You may also purchase workbooks for your bible study.

*JESUS…It's For Him because It's All About Him!*